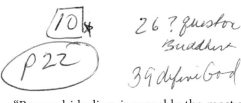

handwritten: 10 *handwritten: P22* *handwritten: 26 ? question Buddhist* *handwritten: 39 define God*

"Personal idealism is arguably the most plausible expression of the bibli-cal documents in metaphysical terms. Ward's new book offers the most convincing exposition of personal idealism I have ever read. One by one, he explores the main challenges to this view, responding to each with ad-mirable sharpness and clarity, then gradually drawing them all together in service of the profound spiritual vision of intimate participation in the divine nature." *handwritten: 83 Aquinas critique of*

—Philip Clayton

handwritten: 94

Author of *The Problem of God in Modern Thought*

handwritten: 10 *handwritten: 79-80 Gregory of Nyssa 80 (book)*

handwritten: 103 Swinburne (book)

"This is a robust defence of a biblical understanding of God against the undue influence of Plato and Aristotle in much Christian thought. Engag-ing with David Bentley Hart, Rowan Williams, and others, Professor Ward argues that creation and incarnation really do affect God. This involves a radical rethink of what we mean by God's impassibility and immutability. Essential reading for all engaged in the philosophy of religion."

—Richard Harries

King's College, London

handwritten: 116 117 118-120

handwritten: 128 see footnote Fides 130

handwritten: 141

"With his vast philosophical and theological scholarship and trademark lucid style, Professor Ward offers us a detailed exposition of the New Testa-ment's teaching on who the God of Jesus is. On this basis, Ward re-exam-ines the dominant Aristotelian-based Western theology of God and finds it deeply wanting. As a 'personal idealist,' Ward articulates an alternative theology of God who has enabled humans to share in the divine nature. This God is a God of creative, redemptive, and sanctifying love. I enthusi-astically recommend this book to all, beginning theology students as well as seasoned scholars."

—Peter C. Phan

Georgetown University

handwritten: Aquinas 142 146

handwritten: Fiddes book atonement p 128 top

handwritten: otherness

handwritten: Westermann "What does the OT say about God" p 34

handwritten: Heshel the Prophet

"This is a rich, profound, and yet accessible book. It is Keith Ward in conversation; his interlocutors are primarily the great theologians and philosophers of the twentieth century. Ward gently chides, explains, and illuminates the nature of the faith. A book that lives with you long after you finish reading it."

—Ian S. Markham
Virginia Theological Seminary

"Never one to shirk the big questions, Keith Ward devotes his new book to a critical analysis of what it means for God to be God. He clearly differentiates his own understanding of Christian theology from the views of those who insist that a maximally perfect God must be simple, immutable, and impassible. Taking his scalpel to Thomist scholarship, he laments its over-dependence on the metaphysics of Aristotle and offers instead a sparkling defence of a God passionately affected by what happens in an alienated and suffering creation, ultimately destined for union in Christ. Innovative and nuanced, *Sharing in the Divine Nature* is an exciting exploration of the respects in which a perfect God may be said to have many unactualized potentialities."

—John Hedley Brooke
University of Oxford

SHARING IN THE DIVINE NATURE

SHARING

IN THE

DIVINE NATURE

A Personalist Metaphysics

―――――――――

Keith Ward

CASCADE *Books* • Eugene, Oregon

SHARING IN THE DIVINE NATURE
A Personalist Metaphysics

Cascade Books
An Imprint of Wipf and Stock Publishers
199 W. 8th Ave., Suite 3
Eugene, OR 97401

www.wipfandstock.com

PAPERBACK ISBN: 978-1-7252-6638-4
HARDCOVER ISBN: 978-1-7252-6639-1
EBOOK ISBN: 978-1-7252-6640-7

Cataloging-in-Publication data:

Names: Ward, Keith, 1938–, author.

Title: Sharing in the divine nature : a personalist metaphysics / Keith Ward.

Description: Eugene, OR : Cascade Books, 2020 Includes bibliographical references and index.

Identifiers: ISBN 978-1-7252-6638-4 (paperback) | ISBN 978-1-7252-6639-1 (hardcover) | ISBN 978-1-7252-6640-7 (ebook)

Subjects: LCSH: Metaphysics. | God. | Open theism. | Christianity—Philosophy. | Theism. | God (Christianity)—Attributes.

Classification: LCC BT102 W21 2020 (print) | LCC BT102 (ebook)

Manufactured in the U.S.A.   APRIL 28, 2020

". . . γένησθε θείας κοινωνοὶ φύσεως . . ."
2 Peter 1:4

Contents

Acknowledgements

I would like to thank my editor, Robin Parry, for his invaluable help in bringing this book to fruition.

I

Metaphysics

GOD WAS IN CHRIST

"God was in Christ, reconciling the world to himself" (2 Cor 5:19). This short New Testament phrase articulated a new and distinctive metaphysics, by which I mean a general systematic account of the nature of reality. For the tradition of Hebrew thought it was a new view of God, one that saw God as being "in" or identified in some way with part of the created universe. It was a view of the "world" (perhaps the whole universe, but especially the human world) as estranged from God. And it was a view of a reconciliation of the world to God, even a uniting of the world to God. That reconciliation would presumably only be completed in future, when all human creatures (who constitute an important part of "the world") would be fully reconciled to God.

It is not co-incidental that this provides a threefold description of God. God is, in accordance with the Jewish tradition, the *creator* of everything other than God. God is actively *present in Jesus* in a unique way. And God *reconciles the world* to God by liberating humans from their condition of estrangement. God is creator, redeemer, and sanctifier, and this is a distinctively trinitarian view of God and of the relation of God to the universe.

1

DOES THE BIBLE ENTAIL METAPHYSICS?

Does the Bible entail metaphysics? My simple answer to this is "yes." I am using the word metaphysics to denote a general account of the nature of reality, and the place of human beings within it. There has been a strange reluctance to admit that Christianity has any metaphysical views. However, the plain fact is that Christianity has many, perhaps too many, such views. If the Bible says that humans are made in the image of God, the God who created the universe, and some or maybe all of them will be resurrected after death, this entails that there is a God and that humans can survive bodily death, that they are like God in some respects, and they have a purpose, which is to relate to God, on whom the whole universe depends. That is a straightforward set of metaphysical beliefs, in the sense I have given. Lots of people reject the view that the universe depends on something other than itself (i.e., that the universe is created), that it has a purpose, and that humans can survive death, but I suppose that the vast majority of Christians accept all these claims, *so they have a metaphysics, whether they know it or not.*

Christians go on to give very different interpretations of the claims mentioned above, which is why there are many Christian metaphysical views. But what can be meant by saying that these beliefs are not central to Christianity? They are not merely speculations, with no investment of desire or interest.

George Lindbeck, in his influential book *The Nature of Doctrine*, distinguished three approaches to Christian doctrine: the cognitive-propositional, the experiential-expressive, and the cultural-linguistic. He argued that doctrinal statements should mainly be understood using the third approach. They are, he suggests, analyses of the grammar of Christian talk, the logic of our language of God. It seems that on this account talk precedes analysis of "grammar," and perhaps praxis—activities such as prayer, ritual or liturgy, and spiritual practice—precedes talk.

I don't think anyone has ever suggested that some theoretician sits down and devises purely rational arguments for a God, and then someone else devises prayers and rituals to accompany those arguments. But it would be even odder to suggest that someone invents prayers and rituals, and later someone else devises grammatical remarks about them.

"Grammar" is itself a very odd term to use about theology. Grammar deals with the correct usage of words, and this changes from one social

2

group to another, and from one time to another. There is no such thing as objectively correct grammar. It either records usage correctly or it does not. Grammarians do not concern themselves with whether linguistic statements are true or false. They only care about whether they are elegantly formed in a specific social context.

Grammarians occasionally try to influence language, but that is generally frowned upon, or seen as an attempt to impose one way of speaking on groups that do not necessarily wish to speak that way (the use of "correct grammar" is often employed to reinforce class privilege). Grammarians do not impose a way of speaking because it is "true," however. Their concern is with privileging a specific social group, whether what that group says is nonsense or sheer fantasy. No doubt there was a correct grammatical way of speaking about spirits and demons in ancient religions. But what they said was false, and that was not a grammatical mistake.

There might be a sort of "grammar of God," a correct way of using the word in a specific community. But that way can and does change, and it does not change just because the group decides it prefers to speak in a different way. For example, it was correct (acceptable) to speak of God as recommending genocide in some Hebrew Bible passages. Later on, and especially with the major prophets and with Jesus, it became unacceptable to do so. But did Jesus just think his Aramaic was preferable to ancient Hebrew? Or was he likely to think that we should no longer think of God as vindictive? If so, that was an *ethical* change, *not a grammatical one.*

Probably, early hominids sacrificed, danced, and sang before they developed a sophisticated language. In that sense, praxis predates theory. But some people began to ask whether there really were spirits, and whether they had causal effects, and could be influenced by really good dances. Theology began. And therefore so did metaphysics—not some grand all-encompassing system into which everything had to fit, but just a list of the kind of things that exist (including whether they were all "things"), and what humans could expect of them when they danced and chanted. Primitive theology looked at practices, and asked, not what their grammar was, but whether they disclosed elements of reality or not, whether the words they used expressed something true (that there are spirits who can heal diseases), or implied things that were untrue.

How can you criticize a practice if you do not ask about truth? I would think that many practices common in Christianity are absurd (I think of opening a window, to let a dying person's soul out—nicely symbolic, perhaps, to a sophisticated theologian, but taken literally by many). To give a symbolic, as opposed to a literal, interpretation, you do not just change the way people speak. You try, where appropriate, to stop people thinking literally, but you hope they will still think grammatically.

Perhaps what objectors to metaphysics mean is that one should not have a purely speculative approach to faith—though they still tend to wish to affirm that the Trinity is three co-equal persons in one substance, which is a metaphysical statement of spectacular obscurity. There is something required of a person of faith that is rarely found and that precedes any speculative thought. That is, *a primary concern for truth and for goodness*. These are value-commitments, and one may well say that the important thing in the life of faith is to aim at those things, and to do so, perhaps, in response to an objective demand for truth and goodness that one has encountered in some personal life-experience. That is not a matter of grammar, nor is it a matter of having some special psychological experience, nor is it a matter of abstract speculation. It is a matter of what is felt to be *an encounter with something of intrinsic and demanding worth*. It is not the quality of subjective experience that is important, but the *object* that one seems to encounter in and through experience. Is there such an object? Ah, that is a *metaphysical* question. To address it is to enter the borderlands of theology.

One simply cannot disconnect truth-claims (the cognitive), experiences, and social practices. One must ask of all social practices (all language-games, in that over-used image often taken out of context from Wittgenstein) whether they disclose truth, or, as they so often do, reinforce ancient prejudices. One must ask of all experiences whether they make any claims about objective reality that cohere with our general views of what is real, and whether they make for universal good, or merely increase personal self-satisfaction. One must ask of all truth-claims whether they have any worthwhile practical impact on one's inner life and social behavior, or whether they are a product of wish-fulfillment or simple inattention to detail.

All these questions are about the *rationality* of religious belief, experience, and practice. Rationality in this sense is not a deductive practice, but an integrative practice. It tries to integrate scientific knowledge, ethics, the arts, worldviews, and spiritual practices (if they are admitted as relevant), so that they together make coherent sense.

I doubt if there is any such thing as what some people have called "secular reason." There is just being reasonable as opposed to being irrational, illogical, or incoherent. Humans being what they are, there will be no agreement on how one interprets these features of the intellectual landscape. Some will argue that only the natural sciences provide knowledge, and all the rest is a matter of wholly subjective opinion. This is not a sort of "secular reason." It is just a particular and rather restricted view of what knowledge is, probably together with a dislike of religious beliefs and practices. Most philosophers who have been called rationalists have in fact believed in God, and in some form of (probably rather unusual) spiritual practice.

Most religious believers are not philosophers, so their primary interest is not in trying to have some coherent framework of well-integrated beliefs. Nevertheless, they will hope that some sort of a framework exists—that is, that their beliefs are not stupid or arbitrary. In this book I develop a specific metaphysical view, which is not shared by all people or even by all Christians, by any means. The more detailed one's metaphysics, the more internally diverse one realizes that Christianity is. Its ideas are always contested by other Christians as well as by unbelievers, and they are always dependent on being framed in particular historical and social contexts.

Does my metaphysics comment on the grammar of some Christian talk, and does it derive wholly from some particular church or is it just from the Bible? Obviously not. My grammar is pretty good, but I am not concerned with that. And the sources of my metaphysical views are many. One source is modern analytical philosophy, which I have taught for many years, and gives me an interest in the uses of language—but in meaning, not syntax. Another is the study of ancient Greek philosophy, which has been used by many Christians to frame a general philosophical view that has sometimes become part of church doctrine. (Transubstantiation, for example, which is apt to be accepted or rejected depending on what one thinks of Aristotle.) The Bible is a major part, though not the only part, of this process of metaphysical reflection. Even though there is no one consistent metaphysics in the Bible, there are general metaphysical assertions—like the existence of a supreme creator—which are present there. I have found the Gospel of John and some New Testament letters particularly illuminating. But my interpretations of the Bible certainly depend on the detailed work of many specialist scholars, though I cannot—no one could—agree with all of them. I would wish my view to be consistent with large chunks of the Bible, and I need good reasons for rejecting other chunks, which I regard as less important or even mistaken (like, for instance, the existence of demons and the coming of Christ on the clouds in the near future).

THE INFLUENCE OF WITTGENSTEIN

For seven years I was Director of Studies in Philosophy at Trinity Hall, Cambridge, and lectured in the Philosophy Faculty. Wittgenstein was still an important philosophical influence, though a very controversial one, in Cambridge at that time. He had a view of philosophy that some called "philosophical behaviorism," though that term is not fully appropriate to describe his complex views. I regard Fergus Kerr's *Theology after Wittgenstein* as one of the best short expositions of Wittgenstein's philosophy, and a fascinating application of it to theology. Certainly, much modern theology has been influenced by Wittgenstein, and I wish to suggest that, though the philosopher has indeed much of interest to say, in the end he does not deal with religious belief in a very satisfactory way. I will support my suggestion by considering and responding to some of the things Kerr says.

Kerr begins with a splendid analysis of what Wittgenstein was protesting about. It was the idea of humans as lonely, atomistic egos, observing the world in a detached, dispassionate way, and inventing words to name objects they perceive in their essentially private and solitary experience. This gives them some firm foundations on which to erect impressive edifices of knowledge. After they have constructed some impressive theories, they (or some of them) go on to start worshipping the God they have invented.

In opposition to all this, Wittgenstein is concerned to stress that humans are essentially social animals, that their languages are parts of their forms of social activity, and language-uses in religion, as in all areas of human life, are expressions of basic social practices that need, and can have, no theoretical or speculative justification.

Words like "soul" and "God" do not refer to specific objects that have perhaps been discerned in some private experience, or that could be discovered by some clever detective work. They are words with some specific *uses* in a "form of life" in which people comfort, console, encourage, and bless or curse one another. We should not ask what those words "stand for," and then ask whether such things exist. We should ask how the words are *used*, and not look behind such social practices to find some invisible metaphysical entities.

Theology is thus "grammar," in the sense that it investigates how words are used in religious contexts, and in ordinary social life. Theology is not a speculative construction out of basically private experiences of

6

the geography of a supernatural world in which the special objects it talks about reside.

One can see why some have called this philosophy "behaviorist"—it moves attention from the foundations of all knowledge in the private experiences of ideally rational observers to seeing how public and social forms of activity generate uses of language that serve specific social purposes. But Wittgenstein claimed to have no metaphysical views, and not to be "reducing" humans to physical objects behaving in certain ways. So it is better to see him as stressing the manifold social uses of language and the ways in which language springs from social needs and practices rather than from the solitary theoretical speculations of solitary minds.

The objects of the Wittgensteinian attack are in part the British empiricist philosophers, John Locke, George Berkeley, and David Hume, and perhaps the earlier Wittgenstein of the *Tractatus Logico Philosophicus* (1921). It is true that they claim to find the foundations of knowledge in the occurrence of "ideas" (or "perceptions" or "sense-data") in the minds of individuals. They do tend to say, as Kerr puts it, that "I enjoy immediate non-linguistic knowledge of my own inner experiences, while what I am experiencing at any moment necessarily remains hidden from other people."[1] This does raise problems, familiar by now, for knowledge of an enduring external world and for knowledge of other minds, and probably they never quite resolved these problems. Something more needs to be said.

It does not seem plausible, however, to deny that there is non-linguistic knowledge, and that it is largely hidden from other people. Examples of such knowledge are many and familiar. Babies know something about their world before they learn to speak. And we just have to guess at what such non-linguistic knowledge is like for a baby. Even adults can have experiences that they have no adequate way of describing or putting into words, and some of the experiences of others can be virtually incomprehensible to us. It would be absurd to say that there are no such experiences, or that we could in principle always come to understand them. That would just show lack of familiarity even with many people who live in the same town as us, not to mention members of very different cultures and historical epochs.

In the religious sphere, the Buddhist experience of *nirvana* is said to be indescribable, and it is certainly not comprehensible to most people. Similarly, those who claim to experience the presence of God are claiming something very hard to describe, that would be rejected as illusion by

1. Kerr, *Theology After Wittgenstein*, 11.

many. Such experiences may be surrounded or even evoked by language, but they are non-linguistically known and hidden from others—there are expressions of them in behavior, but even these expressions are interpreted in very different ways, and different people view them in different ways, from highly esteeming them to seeing them as objects to be ridiculed.

What would be wrong would be to say that all knowledge is built up from private and largely inexpressible experiences. This, I think, is one of Wittgenstein's main points. Conceptual knowledge does not emerge from naming some private experience, and then somehow communicating it to others. (Indeed, how could we be sure there were any "others," who were not just logical constructions from our experiences?) Babies learn languages from others, and they learn them in the context of social activities, like eating, playing games, and being rewarded or punished. Humans are social animals, and knowledge is largely learned from others, not autonomously constructed on one's own.

The empiricists, actually, were well aware that humans are not dispassionate observers. They are agents, moved by passion, and subject to instinctive and often unconscious behavior patterns. They never actually see sense-data and then construct objects out of them. They find themselves acting and changing and responding passionately to stimuli that threaten or please them. At a very early age, they begin to learn to control their bodies and learn how to obtain their goals. The very existence of sense-data is only known (if it is ever known) by a sophisticated abstraction from a rapidly changing experience of threats and gratifications, of actions and reactions, of pleasures and pains, in a continuing flowing process in which they are involved from the first.

Belief in the existence of other minds, other agents, is not an inference. One has to learn to distinguish self from other, what is controllable from what is imposed upon one. This is an interpretation, a beginning of conceptual thought, not an uncertain inference from something better known. It is part of this interpretation that thoughts and feelings are naturally expressed in behavioral ways. If I am in pain, I scream; if I am pleased, I laugh. I do not neutrally observe my pain or pleasure, give them a name, and then announce that name to the world.

Empiricists know this. All the empiricist is saying is that pain or pleasure can exist, whether or not I scream or laugh. Behavior expresses pain or pleasure, naturally but not necessarily. And people quickly learn to dissemble, and conceal their true feelings, with greater or less success (spies are those who are very successful).

To take a religious case: how do we know when prayer is genuine? Prayer is naturally expressed by bodily posture or verbal utterance. But hypocrisy is not uncommon. The correct expression of a prayer does not entail the sincerity of its performance. Only the heart knows if prayer is genuine; and any good Calvinist would say that even the heart may be deceived. Believers regularly say that only God knows the secrets of the heart, and that is certainly not by taking note of people's words or bodily positions.

Where, then, is the dispassionate autonomous lonely ego who is the object of criticism? Not in Kant or Hume, who both wrote sensitively of the passions and of their importance in human life, and who both stressed the importance of considering and respecting others in making moral decisions. It is a rhetorical and almost entirely fictitious construct. There is good reason for empiricists and idealist metaphysicians to see humans as social animals, parts of communities that have histories of developing language uses, fully embodied, learning from and sharing with others. What they have to say does not contradict this, but merely claims that even social animals have private thoughts and feelings. Human animals are distinguished, in standard cases, by being able to stand back and reflect upon their experiences, trying to construct coherent understandings of the nature of human existence and of reality. This can properly be called metaphysics, and it does not need to express "rancour against the physical and historical conditions of human life."[2] Indeed, part of one important metaphysical understanding of human existence is precisely that humans are subject to important physical and historical conditions. They are, however, able to come to understand their own natures better, and that, if it is to include an attempt to understand the many different facets of human life and experience, is in part a metaphysical quest.

It is important to see the physical, communal, and historical conditions of human existence, but attacks on "atomistic detached observers" are aimed at a largely imaginary opponent. Kant, for example, a common object of such criticism, and a self-styled critical idealist, was in fact at pains to say that humans should see themselves as members of a "kingdom of ends." He called for a passionate commitment to moral goals, and held that reasoning is primarily a practice that must always serve the striving for a just and compassionate society. That view is neither atomistic, detached,

2. Kerr, *Theology After Wittgenstein*, 188.

nor purely theoretical. So one objection to many common interpretations of Wittgenstein is that, like Don Quixote, they combat an opponent that they have themselves invented.

A second objection is this: the trouble with taking social practices as not standing in need of justification is that many human social practices are morally questionable and scientifically irrational. If we took theology as an analysis of how words like "God" are used in specific religious communities, we would come across many questionable and/or irrational beliefs. In some religious societies, the word "God" is used to justify killing unbelievers. Would that matter, as long as we had the "grammar" correct? But who decides what grammar is correct, and why should anyone listen to them? How could you ever criticize them? How could reform be possible? Would anyone care if you said, "I think your grammar is atrocious"? And is that really all you would have to say? When some followers of Wittgenstein repeat his words, "language is in order as it is," they neglect the evil, the hatred, and the ignorance that is built into so many human social practices and their associated language-games. Social practices may be prior in time to reflection upon them; but they *do* stand in need of justification. We need to ask what ends they serve, whether those ends stand up to moral scrutiny, and how well existing practices serve them.

If all theologians did was to analyze how people used the word "God," they would end up with a very tedious and long list of uses in innumerable diverse communities, many of which would turn out to be scientifically ill-informed and morally perverse. Critical thinking is needed in theology as in any allegedly cognitive discipline. What one wants to know is whether such a thing as God exists. Now Kerr actually says at one point, "God is not an object."[3] Wittgenstein himself says, "What is here at issue is not the existence of something."[4] For me, this is a very large step too far. Of course God is not literally picturable, but it seems obvious that if the universe is aimed at some goal, and if intrinsic values exist, and if people ever truly sense a personal presence in and through the objects of their experience, one is committed to asserting that *something* exists that has not solely physical properties but that has causal effects on physical reality, something very like God. This is not a remark about grammar.

The final objection that I will mention is that Wittgenstein-influenced views often imply that what is wrong with metaphysics is that it undermines

---

3. Kerr, *Theology After Wittgenstein*, 147.
4. Wittgenstein, *Culture and Value*, 82.

common sense. We should be content with a commonsense view of the world, and not try to replace it with some sophisticated intellectual construction. The objection is that this replacement of commonsense views is precisely what the natural sciences do. The world of quantum physics is almost wholly unlike the world of solid, three-dimensional, colored objects that is the commonsense world. It is unintelligible to most of the world's population, and imperfectly understood by the rest. But few informed people would deny that it is true, or that it is the real basis of how the physical world appears to animals like us. In short, reality is unlike appearance. What is truly real is hidden to most people and obeys mathematical principles that most cannot even understand. The appearance is how the world appears to us, as filtered through our rather small and inefficient brains.

In other words, language is not in order as it is. It may enable us to get by in most everyday situations. But it needs radical re-adjustment and constant criticism if it is to help to build computers and nuclear power stations. What I think this suggests is that we should not be content, if we are seeking truth, with just repeating ordinary language-uses. We should seek the extraordinary. For that, we need the contribution of uniquely creative minds with rare abilities, not a submission to social practices and commonplace beliefs.

Einstein was not a detached and impartial lonely ego. But he was certainly not a conformist to some social practice, and his intellectual work changed the language of physics, and our understanding of the physical world. Of course, he existed in a scientific community, and stood on the shoulders, as he said, of James Clerk Maxwell, and of others too. But what he did was to propound a theory that gave a new, elegant, scientifically fruitful, and very surprising view of what the world is really like. Ironically, Wittgenstein did this too, in the little world of philosophy—even though he claimed to have no metaphysics (where "metaphysics" is again an imaginary opponent). Perhaps we ought to think that ordinary language is never in order as it is, except for purely pragmatic purposes in normal (or what seem to us normal) situations.

Starting from existing theories and problems, Einstein imaginatively pursued thought-experiments that led to relativity theory. He used the public language of mathematics, but he used it in new ways, with new results. It was not that he consulted his private sense-data and gave them names. What he did was to think of large sets of experimental data, use mathematical techniques he had learned, and come up with a new way of understanding gravity. He did this uniquely and against much opposition and even ridicule. He single-handedly changed the language of physics. He worked within a social practice of a very refined sort, and he criticized not its grammar but its content. He solved problems by proposing a worldview of physics that was revisionist, critical, and imaginative, and that claimed that how things really are is not the way they appear.

That, I think, is also what theology does at its best, seeing problems that arise from new knowledge—especially from science, from better understanding of world religions, and from new moral emphases on equality and gender—and trying to incorporate them into a new imaginative picture of how things are. If common sense ignores God, or has an inadequate picture of God, theology tries to present a broader and more inclusive picture of reality, which it believes to be true to the way things are. This may indeed be impossibly ambitious, and is never likely to be wholly successful—all metaphysics is provisional—but it is not grammar, or the study of how words are used. It may change how some words are used, but that will be because the change is believed to give a better insight into reality. In many, but not all, ways theory precedes practice, and that is bound to be the case where issues of truth are at stake.

NON-REALISM IN THEOLOGY

Fergus Kerr gives an excellent exposition of Wittgenstein's thought—though all such accounts are bound to be controversial to some extent. But I think that, to the extent it claims to bypass metaphysics and to found philosophy on description of language-uses rather than on investigations into the truths conveyed by language, it is fundamentally misleading.

Nevertheless, it has been very influential on much modern theology, and among its most influential exponents in the English-speaking world are D. Z. Phillips, Don Cupitt, and Stewart Sutherland.[5] I am not implying that such exponents agree among themselves, but only that they adopt a basically Wittgensteinian approach to religious belief.

A major problem with such an approach is its claim to be free of metaphysics. It does have a metaphysical view, a view of what the real nature of reality is, and of how human lives are to be lived in the light of that. For them, reality has no objective purpose, no goal to which it leads. It does not

---

5. I have commented in detail on the work of Don Cupitt (in *Holding Fast to God*) and Stewart Sutherland (in "Stewart Sutherland: An Appreciation").

depend on a purely spiritual being that lies beyond it. And human beings cannot survive death, as they are purely and inseparably psycho-physical organisms that are doomed to die with their bodily perishing. Admittedly this is not a startling or grand metaphysical theory. It is more like what Peter Strawson called "descriptive metaphysics," and as such it is a form of "naturalism," denying any form of causal interference in the world by a supernatural reality, and any objective purpose for the cosmos.

Yet in the hands of these authors it adds to naturalism a view derived from Wittgenstein that one cannot compare languages to reality to test whether they are true or not. Truth and meaning are decided *within* specific "language-games," and "the criteria of meaningfulness cannot be found outside" such games.[6] Religion has a particular set of language-games. These function within, and are part of, sets of social practices that enshrine ideals and ways of life.

So, on this view, naturalism is true to the extent that there is no extra object that is God and there is no existence after death. But it is false if it says that such a basically scientific account states all there is to reality. There are areas of the aesthetic, the ethical, and the religious, which have their own sorts of reality that cannot be reduced to the physical.

It may be thought that if there is no objectively existing God and no afterlife, there can be no Christian faith. But that, non-realists would say, would be to assimilate religious to scientific language, which is a mistake. Religious language has its own logic, its own "grammar," which is learned by participating in religious practices.

For instance, at a funeral someone may say, "John, though he is dead, has entered into eternal life." When you look at how such statements are used, what their social function is, you see that it is to console, and preserve hope in face of grief. It is not to speculate that he now lives somewhere else, or what exactly he is doing.

"Eternal life is the reality of goodness," writes Phillips.[7] There is a transcendent order of eternal values, to do with self-renunciation and love without possessiveness, and the good things of John's life will always remain in union with that order. There is an eternal goodness; it cannot be defeated by death; and John's was a life that participated in that reality.

This is a metaphysics, which says that what we call "reality" is defined by language, and as there are different sorts of language, there are different

6. See Phillips, *Wittgenstein and Religion.*

7. Phillips, *Death and Immortality*, 48.

sorts of reality. These sorts must not be confused with one another; nor can they be translated into other forms of language. You learn what they mean by participating in groups where they have a particular set of uses.

However, one must admit that scientific, or straightforwardly literal language, is accepted by everyone. It is not just an option. Whereas religious languages are many, vary from group to group, and are wholly rejected by some. How then can one rationally choose between them? Not, on this theory, by finding some external justification, for such does not exist. It seems a matter of whether the religious language in question appeals or not, perhaps of the sort of person one wants to be, or the social group one belongs to.

If people reject such religious groups and languages, they are not disagreeing about facts, but about ways of being in the world, the kinds of thing one thinks are important, authentic, and demanding of our loyalty.

There are huge disagreements in religion, but Phillips writes as though it was quite clear what "eternal values" are, that they involve self-renunciation and love of such things as kindness and humility. It seems that religious language can refer to eternal values and say truly what they are. But there is a problem about referring to values, since on many views, values are not existent things, but are founded on subjective preferences. Phillips seemingly wants to include these values in the contents of reality, and *that is a metaphysical move.* But he wants to make a clear and absolute difference between such reality-references and any physical references.

He says that the ideas of God and of a last judgment, for instance, don't refer to anything. That is not how they are used. "Praying to avoid God's anger is thus not a praying to avoid consequences, but a praying to avoid becoming a certain kind of person."[8] And praying, of course, is just encouraging oneself to avoid that, not communicating with an invisible person.

If words can refer to values, however, why can they not refer to other entities, like God? Is it not in fact rather strange to make a sharp distinction between fact-reference and value-reference, such that we can refer to values but not to a personal being who creates the world? Values, after all, are meant to be incorporated into the world. They specify goals for human endeavor, and adumbrate the sorts of persons we should be. God, too, is not value-neutral. God specifies goals for the universe, and those goals become purposes that persons *ought* to pursue. There is a moral demand,

8. Phillips, *Wittgenstein and Religion*, 246.

arising from the fact that God, for a Christian, is a being worthy of our love and total loyalty, so that we naturally will to do what God, who is a being of supreme value, wills us to do. On the theistic hypothesis, all values are maximally instantiated in one non-physical reality, God. Why could we not refer to that?

It could be said that values have no causal properties, and so cannot influence what happens in physical fact. That is a coherent possibility. It is Aristotle's position, and that of Iris Murdoch. But why could one's religious picture not include a causal element in the supremely valuable being, so that it would influence, and eventually realize in full, the values that it demands of created persons? (I am not talking about truth here, but about conceptual possibility.)

Phillips might say that we could not refer to such a being, but why not? Possibly because, from a scientific point of view, we might think we know the world has no purpose. But that is not a matter of describing the use of religious language. Nor is it a matter of describing how scientific language is used. It is a judgment that scientific language is the only language that has objective reference to physical facts. That is a metaphysical, and highly disputed, judgment. Indeed, any use of such judgments to force a certain interpretation of religious language (that it cannot refer to physical facts) relates empirical and religious languages in a very strong way, since it uses (alleged) science to criticize (alleged) religion.

That too points to the major disadvantage of non-realist (allegedly non-metaphysical) views of religious language. Religious language is not a distinct, clearly defined and bounded type of language—Wittgenstein would probably be the first to protest about such a *priori* boundaries and definitions. If it were, all religious language-games would be immune from criticism and would consist of a number of criterionless options (options because there are many of them, and criterionless because there is no justification of them possible from outside the "games").

That, however, is not how religious believers see their faith. They typically think that their beliefs are both true and subject to criticism on both scientific and moral grounds, though they usually think such criticisms can be defeated. The most obvious example of this in Christianity is the problem of suffering. The facts of suffering (mere facts) do seem to cast doubt on some assertions religion makes about the goodness (mere values) of being. If there is a problem of suffering, it arises from comparing religious language with fact-stating language. On the non-realist theory, they are incomparable. But for many religious believers such a comparison is unavoidable. Facts are relevant to evaluations.

If a non-realist account of religious language was correct, it would not be possible to speak of experiencing the presence of God, as a reality that exists apart from humans, and that humans can come to know in part and be devoted to in love and worship. You would have to mean by such talk that you wanted to become a certain sort of person. Christians do want to become certain sorts of person, but the reason for that is that they want to be more like what they love, and there exists something that they love, and which might help them to be more like that, and might ensure that they could realize such a desire. How, then, can the question of the existence of God not be a factual question, even though it is not an empirically decidable one?

Other features of Christian belief that are important are having a sense of vocation, calling, or specific purposes for one's life. And having a hope for the future triumph of love in the world, and in the possibility of personally sharing in that triumph. But these are all factual matters.

For Phillips there are no such purposes, no such goals, no such triumph. Indeed, he says that to believe in such things would not be properly religious and would somehow be morally suspect (a form of long-term self-interest, perhaps?). However, belief in a loving personal being, in purpose for human lives, and in an achievable goal of supreme worth, in which all can share, is not selfish. It gives hope for people, assuring them that the sufferings they undergo are not the end of the story. There is not only a demanding set of values ("the eternal"), there is the hope that all can share in them, and that even now those values are realized in a being who has ultimate causal influence on events in the world.

The non-realist account of religious belief makes all these things impossible. For such an account, religion is not about facts, and the existence of God is not a factual question.

This is an extremely restrictive view of what "facts" are, and it is an unstable compromise to hold a naturalistic view of the world, while at the same time saying that there really is a transcendent order of values. If you can go so far, it is only one step further to admitting the possible existence of a transcendent God. This case is well argued by Fiona Ellis.[9] It is unsatisfactory to say that metaphysics is impossible, while decreeing that there is no objective purpose in reality, no existent supreme being, and that

9. Ellis, *God, Value, and Nature*.

one should live by commitment to eternal values without hope of reward or success for anyone—assertions that certainly say what reality is really like, and how one should live in the light of that. I would think, however, that there is an implausible gulf between asserting the existence of eternal values and accepting a naturalistic account of factual language. The term "naturalistic" is then extended so far that it is open to assert that other kinds of entities exist, and that they too will be related to physical facts in some way. God may be such an entity, and for many religious believers, that is precisely what God is. Metaphysics is, in any event, *inescapable*. The only question is, *what sort of metaphysics is correct?*

GOD AND MYSTERY

Having defended the possibility and the necessity of having some metaphysical framework for theology, I now aim to show how metaphysics has in fact played an important role in the history of Christian theology. The story of Christian theology can be seen as the story of how believers have tried to work out a coherent and plausible account of biblical teaching in the light of constantly changing (and improving) knowledge of the world and of human nature. Such knowledge does not derive directly from the Bible, though it is arguable that Jewish and Christian traditions both helped to give rise to modern science, and led to moral advances like the abolition of slavery and concern with human rights. It must be acknowledged, however, that there was much opposition to these advances from within the churches, though there never was the total war between science, morality, and religion that some writers have alleged.

The Hebrew Bible, which certainly takes the view that God is the one and only creator, does not, and never intended to, provide a systematic theological account. It was thus natural for Christian thinkers to take concepts that were available in the thought-world of their specific culture and reshape them to construct a conceptual scheme that could fit the new Christian apprehension of God.

The thought-world of the first Christian theologians was very much that of ancient Greece, especially the works of Plato and Aristotle. Philo of Alexandria had already provided a Jewish theological account that used key Greek concepts, and reshaped them to give a systematic doctrine of the God of the Bible. Early Christian theologians naturally used a similar

being, cause, identity
Knowing (posited reality
outside of human sense perception)

scheme, taking concepts from Greek philosophy and trying to adapt them for a distinctively Christian use.

In common with many contemporary Christian theologians, I think that some of these Greek concepts, even when reshaped, gave rise to a one-sided view of God that becomes misleading when it is propagated in the very different cultures of the twenty-first-century world. It also gave rise to unduly paradoxical statements of Christian belief, which a different account can mitigate. The classical theologians regarded these paradoxes as mysteries, and it is important to note that they held the paradoxes to be central to Christian faith.

An example of what I have in mind is that the view of God they developed was that God was simple, immutable, and impassible, but that God also passionately loved and had compassion for creatures. They did not hold that God was immutable in the sense that, like Aristotle's God, God had no knowledge of or relationship to creation. They rather held that God was immutably loving. The paradox, or mystery, was how any being could be *both* unable to change in any respect *and* passionately loving. My view is that this paradox is in fact a contradiction. I do not like contradictions, because there is a simple proof in formal logic that from a contradiction anything whatsoever can be proved—one can prove that God is evil as well as good, for example.[10] I think that the contradiction can be removed without removing a real and important mystery about the being of God.

Gabriel Marcel helpfully distinguished between what he calls a "problem" and a "mystery" by saying that a problem could be solved and understood, whereas a mystery could never be fully comprehended by finite human minds.[11] The being of God is a mystery, because God can never be fully comprehended by human minds, but that does not license one to talk about God in contradictions. I aim to show that some of the classical theological views of God are too near to being contradictions to be secure, and that a non-contradictory view of God can be obtained which preserves a strong sense of mystery—a sense that God cannot be fully understood by human minds.

10. The proof, sometimes quaintly called the principle of explosion, is: Suppose P is both true and false (this is the contradiction). If P is true, then "P or Q" (whatever Q may be—say, "Pigs fly") is true. But if "P or Q" is true, and P is also false, it follows that Q is true. Thus, from any contradiction I can prove that pigs fly.

11. See Marcel, *The Mystery of Being*.

THE METAPHYSICS OF PERSONAL IDEALISM

I shall be commenting on the work of writers on modern theology who give a very different interpretation than mine. In order to keep this book to a reasonable length, I will not be able to mention many modern theologians whom I admire, and who have influenced my thought. I say very little about those with whom I broadly agree, since they have said it so well. I should mention, however, the book *The Openness of God,* by Clark Pinnock and others, which states a view very like the one I outline in this book. It will become apparent that I do not accept the authors' relational view of the Trinity, their claim that if the world is necessary that implies some deficiency in God, and that I have a much greater commitment to the idea of *theosis,* the inclusion of all things in Christ, which is a key theme of this book. But their book, espousing views held by a number of contemporary philosophers and theologians, outlines a distinctively modern approach with which I am in total sympathy. The writers I do talk about, however, are certainly among the theologians that I most admire in modern times, and their writings have a spiritual depth that I have learned much from. Yet I have chosen them precisely because I disagree quite strongly with some of their theological views. I think the reason is most basically that I belong to a way of doing philosophy that is very different from theirs (in most cases they are Thomists or strongly influenced by Thomas Aquinas). I do think that Aquinas is one of the greatest theologians of all time. From my philosophical viewpoint, however, his work has a primary defect, which is that it takes Aristotle too seriously. The differences I have with the writers I shall discuss are philosophical, not based on any scriptural revelation.

I regard Aristotle as an amazingly profound philosopher, but as one many of whose views have failed to withstand the criticisms of subsequent generations of philosophers. While he was an astoundingly acute early scientist, his views on physics, for example, are almost all rejected by modern physicists, and are of historical interest only. Many modern philosophers, myself among them, would say the same of many of his philosophical views. Many of the theses of Aristotelian philosophy are widely rejected by professional philosophers these days, and I think it would be a pity if the statements of Christian theology tied themselves too closely to such a philosophy. One consequence will be that Christians who are looking for a coherent intellectual backing for their faith may find themselves in a small sub-culture of the philosophical world which fails to communicate meaningfully to the general educated population.

I am aware that Christian faith itself may be said to be a small sub-culture of the intellectual world today. I am also aware that there is no generally accepted philosophical system that has a hope of replacing the impressive—but to many people unintelligible—edifice of thirteenth-century Thomism. All I aim to do is to point out what many people outside the Aristotelian thought-world find difficult or unacceptable in that philosophy. I will also have the temerity to suggest an alternative way of giving a coherent interpretation of Christian faith for those who generally accept the ideas of modern science (especially advances in astronomy and evolutionary biology), who are sympathetic to the moral changes in many societies in attitudes to women, animals, the environment, and matters of justice, punishment, and human rights, and who are open to a different philosophical approach.

I do not speak from a neutral philosophical position. I am a *personal idealist*, and I will explain what I mean by this, but I accept that this is a sub-culture too. So I am not saying that some form of Thomism is clearly wrong. I am saying that it does not speak to me or to many people who are unable to accept some of its key claims. My remarks may seem mainly critical, but they are really just ways of explaining why I feel alienated from the philosophical terms, both Thomist and in vocabulary influenced by ancient Greek thought, in which much Christian theology has been expressed. What I wish to do, therefore, is to find a way of accepting most of the practical and spiritual insights that these contemporary theologians undoubtedly have, but disconnecting those insights from an Aristotelian/Thomist philosophy.

As I say, my view is a form of personal idealism.[12] I use the term "idealism" in a very broad sense, to mean that *mind is the ultimate reality, and that the physical world would not exist without mind as its source.* In an important way the material universe is both purposive—it has a goal—and exists for the sake of realizing states and processes that are worthwhile for their own sake. Such states would include things like the creation and appreciation of art, literature, and music; the understanding of natural science and mathematics; and the experience of happiness in the love of others. Such things, in their immense variety, can be seen as forms of experiencing

12. I outline this metaphysical view more fully in *More Than Matter?* and in *The Christian Idea of God.*

realities that can be greatly valued just because of what they are. They are intrinsic values—not means to something greater, but valuable in themselves. Such values are inseparable from the existence of mind, since they only become actual, as opposed to possible, values when they are valued by a conscious and evaluating subject.

I am not adopting the extreme form of idealism that says that nothing but mind exists, and that matter is an illusion. For me, matter is a positive expression of mind, rather as the human body is the expression of the human mind—though this analogy should not be taken too literally. Matter is real, but it is real as a genuine appearance of an underlying and primary reality of a conscious, intelligent, purposive reality.

Those theologians and philosophers who take a different approach either say that there can be no minds without matter, or that God is as different from mind as God is different from matter. They could, of course, say both of these things. By contrast, I think that matter is a natural expression of mind, so maybe minds, maybe even the mind of God, naturally express themselves in a material universe. But even in that case, minds are not accidental by-products of a material universe, as some philosophers hold. In the human case they are intended goals of the material process, and they evolve from matter, though by conscious design, not by accident. The material universe as a whole is a product of one supreme mind, the mind of God, which creates the physical universe to realize many sorts of intrinsic values. Without that mind, the universe would not exist.

Many theologians think that to call God a mind is to make God limited and finite. Minds are finite realities, and God the creator is not like any finite reality. They would not, I think, deny that it is correct to speak of God as knowing, intending, and acting—all of them mental activities. But they would deny that these terms give anything like an adequate idea of God. God is, they say, as far beyond mind as God is from matter. In a way, this is true; God is not just a mind like a finite created mind. God is no doubt infinitely more, and that more we are unable to conceive adequately or imagine. Nevertheless, I think that to speak of God as knowing, feeling, and intending is simply true, whereas to speak of God as sitting on a throne or being like a rock is to use metaphors, utterances that are false in their primary sense. We do not know what it is like for God to know, feel, and intend. It must be very different than it is in the case of human minds, which are for the most part confined to physical brains. But we still have correct knowledge of God when we speak of God thinking and acting. I

21

hope to show that to deny that God is mind (and more) is provocative, counter-intuitive, and unhelpful—or so it seems to me.

Many idealist philosophers go on to claim that though there is in a sense a cosmic mind, it is impersonal. It may have the character of intelligence and bliss, but it is not a being that can or would wish to enter into personal relationships with created minds. As a mind that includes the whole universe it is beyond any sort of mutual relationship with finite minds. In some systems of idealism, finite minds have the aim of being ultimately absorbed into the one universal mind, and transcending all sense of individual reality.

I believe that in the Christian faith finite personal individuality always remains important, so that the ultimate goal is not the transcendence of personality, but its fulfillment in conscious relationship to other minds, creating and sharing values together. Even if the mind of God does in one way include the whole universe, it most fully expresses its inner nature in conscious relationship to minds that are other than it. In the sort of Christian view I accept, the goal of creation is not the realization of the undifferentiated unity of all things, but the realization of a community of individual minds, united indeed, but united by love, not by some sort of merging of identities.

Personal idealism of this sort holds that the cosmic mind expresses its inner nature in conscious relationships of love with minds that are truly other than it, but that are wholly dependent upon it, and that fulfill their natures by their relationship to it. For Christians, God is not a *finite* person, but in the incarnation a finite person becomes a true image of the divine nature, of what the universe in its basic and fully unveiled reality is like. And through the active power of the divine Spirit working within the lives of created minds, those minds can realize their positive potential in fuller relationships, both with other created minds and with the supreme mind of all. In that process, it may be said that even the supreme mind realizes the potential of its own innermost nature as love, as real conscious relationship and communion.

Many theologians in recent times have seen the strength of such a view, but have tried to combine it with views of God as wholly self-contained and complete without the existence of any created universe. This sets up a tension between saying that God has the nature of self-giving and relational love, and maintaining a belief that God is one and wholly self-sufficient. Some try to set up a set of loving relations within the being of God, and say that is what the Trinity is. It is hard to see how there can be conscious relationship and communion within a being that is, when all is said and done, just one mind and will. There may be some sort of love within a unitary God (like Plato's love of the good, also accepted by Aristotle, which is the changeless contemplation of the perfection of the divine nature). But if one is to speak of love as care for that which is truly other, and even for that which is both other and imperfect (that's us!), it is hard to see how such a thing could be included in the being of God itself. To the extent that the nature of God includes such radical self-giving love, it seems that it must realize that nature by relation to a created world of free morally choosing minds. Then the Christian affirmation that "God is love" (1 John 4:8, 16) will entail that God creates and relates personally to minds other than its own. And that in turn entails that God is not completely unknowable, but is a supreme mind that can be truly known and loved by creatures.

God relates personally
to minds other
than its own →

God cares
how we know this?

2

The Aristotelian Legacy

INEFFABLE? DENYS TURNER: THE APOPHATIC WAY

A modern theologian who says, at least some of the time, that God is unknowable is Denys Turner. He has written that Christians must "simultaneously affirm and deny all things of God."[1] His arguments are subtle and ingenious, but I am not convinced. He might, I suspect, regard me as a "rationalist," maybe even worse, a victim of Enlightenment prejudices about language. Accepting that he may be right, I find that I cannot escape my own beliefs on these matters, and all I can do is register what I find unconvincing about what he says so elegantly.

The idea that God is radically "other," so unlike anything created that we must deny even our distinctions between real and unreal when talking of God, goes back at least as far as Dionysius (pseudo-Denys), Meister Eckhart, and Nicholas of Cusa.

I have no trouble with saying that God cannot be *adequately* described or understood in any human language. We could say as much about the physical world described by quantum physicists. Yet in physics there are certainly many true things said about the sub-atomic world, things that are not only true but are well-established by repeated experiments. When, in this physical world, we speak of reality as unknown, even perhaps unknowable,

1. Turner, "Apophaticism, Idolatry and the Claims of Reason," 20.

24

we mean that we cannot picture what objective physical reality is really like in itself, or what it is that makes our statements about indeterminacy or entanglement true. That they are true we do not doubt (though we hope our statements may be improved as knowledge grows). But most of us have renounced the ambition to say that we have a completely adequate understanding of what sub-atomic reality is like.

Is language about God like that? I suspect that it is, that there are many statements about God that we regard as true, even though we have no adequate understanding, no coherent picture or fully coherent theoretical scheme, that can explain what it is in the being of God that makes them true.

It is very important to see this, and it is of great pastoral value to see that different linguistic descriptions of divine reality are not quite as complete and exclusive and hard-edged as some people think. Some people can say that God is a "person," and others may say that the ultimately real is impersonal, yet they may both accept that they are trying to describe in inadequate and culturally influenced ways a reality that may well be the same. Of course, if God is beyond description, they will never know whether they are speaking of the same reality or not. What they cannot say is that both sorts of description are equally adequate, that it does not matter which one we accept, or that nothing is at stake in our different and admittedly inadequate descriptions.

Is Denys Turner saying more than this? My difficulty is that from what he says I cannot be sure, and he has certainly modified his early views in some ways. Part of what he wants to do is to rehabilitate metaphysics as an important implication of any plausible theological view, and I agree totally with that. He rightly says that the main point in talking of God is not a purely theoretical one, but is about the sort of life we live, the attitudes we take to that life, and the sorts of values we find in it and seek to live by. He writes that the goal of the contemplative Christian life is "to be inserted participatively into a darkness of God . . . to be drawn into a sharing in its nature as love, so as to share it in friendship with God."[2]

I agree again. But how do we come to believe that God is love, or that we can share in that love, or, even more dramatically, that we can be "friends with God"? These are things that many theists would not say, that Buddhists would certainly not say. And when we come to ask what sort of love we are thinking of, and we say, perhaps, that it is *agape* or self-sacrificial

2. Turner, "Apophaticism, Idolatry and the Claims of Reason," 30.

love, we find ourselves at odds with many other very devotional forms of theism (like Gaudiya Vaishnavism and some forms of Judaism) that find this impossible to accept. For them, divine love cannot be self-sacrificial, since the divine perfection cannot be qualified, even by a divinely willed decision.

I suppose many Christians would answer that we know that God is love because of the teaching and the life of Jesus. This is an understanding of God that seems to transform some beliefs that were dominant in Jesus' day, and to plant the thought of a suffering God deep in the Christian psyche as a quite new and distinctive revelation. But at this point many non-Christian devout believers in God would honestly think that Jesus was a mistaken apocalyptic miracle-worker and exorcist, and as such is not a reliable guide to the nature of God. Would it then be enough to say that since God is unknowable there is no way of knowing whether Jesus was mistaken or reliable?

We could, I think, reasonably say that there is no way of demonstrating to the satisfaction of every intelligent and informed person, either historically or philosophically, that Jesus was an authentic revelation of God or that he was not. I am not suggesting that there is some prior knowledge of God that could help us to make a definite decision about this. My suggestion is that if you do make a decision you are claiming that some people know in a privileged way something true of God. Many Buddhists will claim that the Buddha knew by personal experience that there is no God, since he knew that all is transient and without substantial foundation. Many Christians will claim that Jesus knew by personal experience that there is a God, since he knew God in a uniquely intimate way (Matt 11:27). They may well add that in his resurrection Jesus stood in the very presence of God. They may also add, if they are bold, that we know that God in Godself is a Trinity of persons, all co-equal and eternal, even though this is never stated in that form in Scripture, and it is hard to see what personal experience could confirm it. If it is said that God has verbally communicated it to some church council, then we are committed to saying that God has revealed something true about God that was formulatable in some human language. Or are we to say that this claim, too, must be denied?

Most Christians will accept the Gospel accounts on faith, but they accept them as giving new, surprising, even counter-intuitive, information about God, that was obtained by the personal experience of Jesus, who is taken to know God in an especially intimate way. How, then, can they regard God as unknowable? How can they say, with Aquinas, that "we are made one with [God] as to something unknown"?[3]

Professor Turner is well aware of these points, and he stresses that the apophatic way of denial must be balanced by the cataphatic way of affirmation. The more positive way moves, as he says, in a progressive hierarchy of attributions from metaphorical statements like "God is a rock," through statements like "God is a great intelligence" to the most general class of statements like "God is good" or "God exists." But if God is unknown, how can such a hierarchy be established? It implies that God is more like goodness and wisdom than God is like a rock. If, like Aquinas, you object to saying that God is like anything finite, we must at least say that goodness and wisdom are more adequate descriptors of God than such properties as solidity and mass.

The hardened atheist will say that there is nothing that is not part of the universe and is more like wisdom than like a rock. In fact, there is in the universe no purpose or goal that some intelligence may have chosen, and there are in the universe no objective values (values that are intrinsically good, whether or not any humans exist or think there are such values). Such an atheist will, in other words, reject the cataphatic way altogether. But Denys Turner argues that without the cataphatic way the assertion of apophaticism has no linguistic role to play. Thus he says, for instance, discussing the "five ways" of Aquinas, that there is a "divine creative causality) which must be incomprehensible to us."[4] He does not say that there is no divine creative causality. He certainly (I think) would not say that "God is *not* a loving savior" *tout court*, as a Buddhist would. It looks as though he ought to be linguistically compelled to say that there is a loving creator and savior, only we cannot fully comprehend or picture what it is like to be such a one. Does this justify him in saying that God is "in unutterable Otherness, beyond the reach of absolutely everything we say"?[5] I think there is a mistake here, which is to think that if you can say anything about an object to which you refer, then what you say must provide a fully adequate description of that object. That, however, is clearly false. I can successfully refer to Theresa May, and say that she used to be Prime Minister of the UK, without knowing anything else about her. If you say, "That's a very inadequate description," *of course* that is the case! I may not even know what a

3. Aquinas, *Summa Theologiae*, 1a, qu. 12, article 13, ad. 1.
4. Turner, "Apophaticism, Idolatry and the Claims of Reason," 29.
5. Turner, "Apophaticism, Idolatry and the Claims of Reason," 32.

Prime Minister is, or what the UK is, or what age Theresa May is. But I have *still* said something true.

Could we say that something exists that we have no words to describe, which is beyond all our linguistic categories? "Whereof we cannot speak, thereof we must be silent," as Wittgenstein's *Tractatus* notoriously concludes. It may be possible to be acquainted with something without having any words to describe it. In such a case, one might be able to give the context in which that experience occurred, or to show the process of thought that led up to it, and perhaps the consequences that flowed from it. Perhaps it was in the context of prayer, during which one was contemplating the power and majesty of the universe, and it left one with a feeling of peace and happiness. Yet this sounds very like the state of *satori* in some types of Buddhism, and there it would not be called God. If God is unknowable, one would have no way of knowing whether or not *satori* and the beatific vision were the same or different. Yet they carry very different expectations about what the universe is like, and they are described in very different, even conflicting, ways.

God is generally thought to be God, whether or not anyone ever experiences God, whether or not there is any universe at all. God is thought to be that which generates the universe from the divine being alone. These, I take it, are meant to be true statements. If so, it is false that we must deny that "there is any kind of thing that God is."[6] God is the kind of thing which is the one and only creator of the universe, which does not depend on anything else for its existence. I may not even be theoretically certain, as a paid-up philosopher, that such a concept makes sense. I have no idea what it is like to be that kind of thing. I cannot imagine it or explain it. But I can say it and claim to know it. I can, and probably should, say that when I contemplate these thoughts, I realize that God is far beyond the limits of my comprehension. But it is not true that I claim to know nothing about God at all.

Part of the difficulty here is the vagueness of the word "thing." God is not a thing in the sense of a part of the universe that can be identified by pointing. But God is a thing, in the sense that the word "God" does have reference, and can be identified by description (even if the description is "that which is beyond all our linguistic categories, though some categories are more adequate than others").

---

6. Turner, "Apophaticism, Idolatry and the Claims of Reason," 20, (quoting Dionysius, *The Divine Names*, 817B, in *Pseudo-Dionysius, The Complete Works*, 98).

Apophatic - obtained through negation

I suspect Denys Turner will agree. He has a footnote complaining that those who have accused him of denying that there can be true statements about God have misunderstood him. Such true statements, he says, "Fail, not of truth but of God."[7] I take this to mean that they are true, but fail to say adequately what God is. My complaint is only that I find it very misleading to say that God is "unutterably Other," if we also wish to say that Jesus is the visible image of the invisible God. If we say both at once, then we should be aware that this is a rhetorical device that precludes us from saying one of these things by itself, as a correct description of God.

Historically, one of the major sources for a belief that God is radically ineffable is Dionysius the Areopagite. Some, such as John Hick and sometimes Denys Turner, have taken Dionysius to say that there is *nothing true* that one can say of God, and the ultimate reality is *completely beyond* all our linguistic categories. But Timothy Knepper, in *Negating Negation*, has argued, by close attention to the relevant texts of Dionysius, that "the Dionysian corpus does not negate all things of an absolutely ineffable God."[8] When Dionysius speaks of the "divine names," he speaks of "the divine causes of the intelligible properties in which beings participate."[9] The divine names in question are such names as "good," "being," "life," and "wisdom." These would have been familiar to Dionysius as the first emanations or "henads" from the Neoplatonic "One." They are the causes of "the basic contours of reality," and as such they utterly transcend those qualities as they exist in created beings, yet also "pre-eminently pre-contain properties in a . . . hyper-existent manner."[10] That is to say, they *really are true* of God, though in a hyper-existent manner. They are not just inapplicable to God.

I do not want to enter into the details of Dionysian scholarship, which is the well-guarded province of several major scholars. But I think what Dr. Knepper is basically saying is that Dionysius never denies that God is the creative cause of all things, so God must be regarded as the cause of being, life, and wisdom. Dionysius would assume that the cause must be greater than, not less or completely other than, the effect. So God must be existent, living, and wise, even if in a "hyper" way. Whether or not this is a correct interpretation of Dionysius, I believe the point to be logically valid, that in order to refer to the Christian God at all one must believe that God is the

7. Turner, "Apophaticism, Idolatry and the Claims of Reason," 16 n. 9.

8. Knepper, *Negating Negation*, ix.

9. Knepper, *Negating Negation*, xii.

10. Knepper, *Negating Negation*, 36.

cause of all, and is of supreme goodness. In that case, it will simply be true that God is living and wise, though it is important to add that what it is *like* for God to exist and be wise is not comprehensible to us. I doubt that it is very helpful to say that we have a "hyper-noetic" understanding of God "that surpasses our ordinary rational and intellectual powers."[11] For me, that is too reminiscent of a gnostic approach to God, which appeals to the special intuitions of a spiritual elite. There may be a spiritual elite (presumably Jesus was a member), but his understanding is not available to us, and what he taught was not that we should have a "hyper-noetic" understanding, but that we should accept that God really is a loving Father. I find it sufficient to say that it is just straightforwardly true that God is wise (which entails, among other things, that God has a good reason for everything God does), though we have very little grasp of what those reasons might be, or how they are experienced by God.

In any case, if one were to accept a completely apophatic concept of God, one could not say that one knows God to be changeless, in the sense of being unaffected by contingent events in the universe, and simple, thus as having no inner complexity at all. One would simply not know whether or not God was changeless and simple. If *all* terms have to be denied of God, so do their contradictories, so God would not be changing and complex, but God would not be changeless and simple either. As Nicholas of Cusa said, if God is "aliud," God is also "non-aliud." When generalized, this entails that if God is not changeable, then God is also not changeless. If neither category fits God, it will not be possible to deduce any particular conclusions from the assertion of God's changelessness, or from an assertion of change in God either. It will rather become incumbent upon us to ask in what respects it is more adequate to speak of God as unchanging, and in what respects as changing. Both will "fail of God," but may be true in some sense. The theological task is to spell this out as coherently as possible.

Of that which no one can understand, no one can dispute. It is probably very useful indeed to remember that, and I think Professor Turner has that to teach us. I also think it follows that what we do understand of God is likely to be very partial and inadequate, and that also I wholeheartedly accept. I am just not as sure as some theologians apparently are of what is meant by God's changelessness, and I do not think that a rather positive assertion of immutability (positive in that it asserts positively that God is

11. Knepper, *Negating Negation*, 106.

ok

not changed by anything in the world) is entailed by the proper ineffability
of God.

so is not a wonderful quality to have.

GOD AS WHOLLY OTHER

Thomas Weinandy, a Franciscan priest and distinguished academic, does
not go as far as Denys Turner in saying that everything can be both affirmed
and denied of God. But he does characterize God as the "wholly other." This
term has its antecedents in early writings on the borderlands of Christian
orthodoxy. More recently it surfaces in Rudolf Otto's description of God as
mysterium—unlike anything in the created world—and it may be justified
by reference to a verse in Isaiah 40:18: "to whom, then, will you liken God,
or what likeness compare with him?" It was also used by Karl Barth as a
way of saying that philosophy could not arrive at a correct concept of God,
and such a concept should wholly depend upon revelation. Barth typically
also, later, spoke of "the humanity of God," which qualifies any assertion of
"radical otherness" in a decisive way.

Of course, God is not exactly like anything in the created physical
universe, since it is generally accepted that God does not have physical
properties. But it is very difficult to say that X is *totally* different from everything else, that there are *no* respects in which God is anything like anything
else. That would mean that there is no general description available to us
under which the concept of "God" would fall, not even such a very general
description such as, "Something that exists." One may want to say that God
does not exist *in the same way* as anything else, but if "exists" means "has
a place in the list of things that are not imaginary, illusory, or fictitious"
then it must be true (or false) that God exists. In that respect it *is* like other
things that exist, that have being whether or not anyone thinks they have
being.

There are theologians who have said "God does not exist." But they
would not say, "There is no God," or "There is nothing I am praying to," so
it seems that they mean that God does not exist *in the same way* that finite
physical things exist. The Hebrew Bible does assert that there should be
no physical images of God, but it is filled with accounts of God revealing
himself, through angels and burning bushes, or in silence after a whirlwind,
and speaking to and through Moses and the prophets. Whatever it is that
does such things, it certainly exists (if they are not illusions). So, I am very
wary of describing God as "wholly other."

When Dr. Weinandy explains what he means by calling God "wholly other," he says that God "cannot be numbered among the things created,"[12] and adds that "in this sense only do I mean that Yahweh is completely and absolutely other." If that is true, this use of "wholly other," though I think the word "wholly" is misleading, is innocuous. God is not a created thing. This idea of God is compatible with biblical writings. But actually Dr. Weinandy builds a number of other features into his idea of God. He espouses a Thomist view of God, carefully defined in the *Summa Theologiae* 1a, articles 2–11, as simple, perfect, limitless, changeless, and timeless. This gives a more limited sense to "wholly other" as meaning: distinguished from any complex, finite, changing, temporal thing. The underlying assumption is that all complex, changing, and temporal things are created things, and that is why God cannot possess these attributes.

David Burrell provides a justification for this, as it seems to me, rather restrictive notion of God, holding that the ideas of divine simplicity and eternity (timelessness) are essential if one is to make a clear distinction between the creator and creation. He insists that God is not just "the biggest thing around."[13] "The one who begins and is the end all things is not one of those things."[14] That is clearly true. But that does not mean that God is not a "thing," an object, a member of the class of "things that exist." All one needs to say is that God is a being who creates everything other than itself, that God is uncreated and uncreatable, since God exists by necessity. This clearly distinguishes God from all created things, though it does not lead to saying that God is not a thing at all.

Burrell quotes Aquinas, who says that God is not a substance, does not belong to a more general genus of things (e.g., gods), and that there is no distinction between God's essence and God's existence; God is not an existent thing, for God is *ipsum esse per se subsistens*, the infinite "to-be," existing in itself. This standard Thomist position is one that I will consider and criticize in some detail at a later stage. I can say now that there is an alternative account, often taken in the history of philosophy, especially since Descartes, and I think a clearer one. It is to say that God is in fact the *primary* substance, the only truly *self-subsistent* thing who falls under the description of "creators of everything but themselves," a class that has only one possible member. As a substance, God has a nature (an essence),

12. Weinandy, *Does God Suffer?* 46.

13. Burrell, "Distinguishing God from the World," 5.

14. Burrell, "Distinguishing God from the World," 6.

which is to be maximally knowing, wise, good, and powerful. This nature, uniquely, is necessarily instantiated (i.e., it exists in every possible world).[15] There remains a logical distinction between God's essence and God's existence though no real, or ontological, separation between them is possible (one can say "there is a possible world that does not contain God" without contradiction, but such a world is not metaphysically possible). The divine nature is then logically complex, comprised of distinct attributes, which are inseparably united, and that is what "simplicity" can be taken to mean.

Burrell wants a stronger sense of "simplicity," such that God's essence is simply "to-be," and is in this sense identical with God's existence. In this, he follows Aquinas, who thought that "Being" or "To-be-ness" is somehow an active principle that generates all beings that exist, that it is itself the maximal case of all perfections (as stated in the fourth of the five ways of demonstrating the existence of God in the *Summa Theologiae*), and that divine self-contemplation (which entails divine knowledge and love of perfect goodness) naturally issues in some creation (goodness naturally diffuses itself). When Aquinas speaks of God as "Being," he is thinking of an absolute fullness of being and creative perfection. He is, in my view, building many other important properties into the abstract notion of "Being." But for me, this view still omits many of the most important properties of a perfect being. I believe that having "fullness of being" entails the capacity for bringing new states into existence, and that entails the existence of potency, in fact unlimited potency, always held within the actuality of the primal source of beings. If we think of God as a maximally perfect agent who acts contingently (and Burrell does say that God acts "gratuitously," which he contrasts with acting "necessarily") in creating this world, we are certainly distinguishing God from the world in a clear way. But this definition in no way entails that God is beyond change, beyond any sort of time, and absolutely simple.

One can therefore question Burrell's rather dogmatic statement that a creator would necessarily have to be simple and timeless. There could be a non-created thing that was complex, changing, and temporal. God

---

15. The idea of possible worlds is generally thought to be found classically in Leibniz, and has been advocated in modern philosophy by Saul Kripke. A "world" is a set of possible entities that can co-exist. In this sense, it may include God, a non-finite existent, but may exclude the "world" in which there are no entities at all (the "null class," a possible world where nothing is possible!). I agree with Leibniz that a maximally knowing God would know all possible worlds, and to say that "God is necessary" is to say that there is no possible world in which God does not exist.

could be such a thing. Whether or not God is such a thing needs to be discussed. At least at first sight, the biblical view of God is of a being who is complex and changing. God is described as having various diverse and complex emotional reactions to human conduct—God hates sin, grieves over sinners, and rejoices in the smell of a good sacrifice. And God changes divine decisions in response to human prayer—as with Abraham and the destruction of Sodom, or Jonah and the destruction of Nineveh, or Moses and the destruction of the Israelites in the wilderness.

SIMPLE?

Metaphor and Analogy

Thomas Weinandy's argument is that Old Testament ideas of God are quite consistent with, and indeed sympathetic to, a Thomistic concept of a simple and changeless God. This is a bold and counter-intuitive claim. If one is talking about the God and Father of Jesus Christ, since Jesus was brought up in the Jewish faith, it is reasonable to start by considering what the Hebrew Bible says about God. It would be useless to go over ground that has already been covered in impressive depth by Old Testament scholars. From a Christian standpoint, Claus Westermann's *What Does the Old Testament Say about God?* is a reliable guide. From a Jewish standpoint, Abraham Heschel's *The Prophets* is instructive. Richard Rice's paper on biblical descriptions of God (in Pinnock et al., *The Openness of God*) is well worth reading. For a general account that is incisive and clear, and the result of years of scholarly work, John Barton's *The History of the Bible* is a lapidary resource.

It is obvious that many statements about God in the Old Testament are metaphorical, and not to be taken at face value. But even metaphors logically entail some straightforwardly factual statements about God. And those statements imply that God is not wholly different in every respect from any created thing. For instance, the statement "God is a rock" is false in its primary and most straightforward meaning. It points to some meaning that is suggested by words like "rock," but it is not at all specific or precise about what those suggestions might be. In this case, we might think that God is being regarded as strong or enduring, but other meanings might suggest themselves. If someone said, "God is not a rock," they would not be mistaken. They may mean that the statement is not literally true, or that they do not appreciate that metaphor. In any case, they would not strictly be contradicting the statement "God is a rock." They would rather be regarding it as inadequate or misleading in some way, which it may be for some people.

I am not suggesting that metaphors can be translated without remainder into literally true assertions. The whole point of metaphors is that they free the imagination to think of many possible connotations and linguistic links, and are not usually tied to just one possible precise meaning.[16] Yet metaphors do necessarily entail there are some meanings that are not themselves metaphorical. It is not possible for every statement about God to be metaphorical. In the case given, if God's rock-likeness is taken by someone to mean (among other things no doubt) that God is strong, then the statement "God is strong" (stronger than any human, say) is just straightforwardly true, and not at all metaphorical. Some statements—however inadequate as full definitions of God, and however much they are implied rather than stated—must be just literally true, if talk of God, however metaphorical, is to have meaning. If God exists, and is stronger than a human, then while God is not a created thing, God has some properties that created things have (i.e., strength).

Aquinas apparently accepts this, holding that "the perfections of everything reside in God."[17] They do so "in a more perfect manner" (*eminentiorem modum*). This seems to entail that God is not only complex, but supremely complex, containing all actual and possible perfections (good states). Aquinas says, "Perfections therefore which are diverse and opposed in themselves, pre-exist as one in God."[18] This notion of divine simplicity seems to mean that the perfections are indivisibly united. A very unconvincing example of the sun is used by Thomas, suggesting that the sun contains the qualities of all the things it causes (including everything on earth), but is in itself primordial and without diversity. The sun has a "unity of nature," and cannot be decomposed into separate parts, but it causes many things which are then separable in their being. Allowing for the fact that this remark about the sun is both false and misleading, scientifically speaking, it may suggest some idea of the source of all created beings as an indivisible totality of all perfections in their highest form. This is very like Plato's idea of the good as the supreme form. It depends upon two philosophical

---

16. A helpful account of metaphors in religion is given in Soskice, *Metaphor and Religious Language*.

17. Aquinas, *Summa Theologiae*, 1a, 4, 5.

18. Aquinas, *Summa Theologiae*, 1a, 4, 3.

dogmas: that causes must be like but greater than their effects, and that unity is preferable and ontologically prior to diversity. It would not be absurd to think that the development of the idea of one supreme God, which was fully formulated by the major biblical prophets like Isaiah, and the related idea that God was the greatest of beings, are sympathetic to these philosophical dogmas, as Dr. Weinandy suggests. Yet if simplicity means "is not composed of separable parts," that does not entail that there are no diverse properties in God. On the contrary, all positive properties, however diverse, must be in God, though as such they cannot be separated out. They form parts of the one indivisible unity of the divine nature. This is a strong reason for resisting an expression like "wholly other" as applicable to God.

Absolute Simplicity

Norman Kretzmann and Eleanor Stump wrote a paper on "Absolute Simplicity," which gives a scholarly and rigorous defense of a Thomist idea of God as one timeless, changeless, and absolutely simple God. As it provides one of the best expositions of this view, and as I disagree with it almost completely, it provides an excellent way of expounding my own very different view, and of exploring the relationship of the two views.

Stump and Kretzmann are distinguished Aquinas scholars, and I can only admire their exposition of Aquinas on this topic. My concern is not with their exegesis of Thomas but with the use of Aristotle and Aquinas to help in formulating a coherent idea of God.

In the article, they take it is an obvious assumption that "In virtue of being absolutely perfect God has no unactualized potentialities." That is not at all obvious to me. The notion of absolute perfection is one with which I have much sympathy. I am inclined to accept Anselm's formula that "God is that than which nothing more perfect can be thought." My reservations are with Anselm's assumption that concepts like "beauty," "wisdom," and "love" are intrinsically worthwhile values (perfections) that objectively exist, and can be objects of contemplation. Diotima's speech in Plato's dialogue *The Symposium* puts this idea very well: "Begin with examples of beauty in this world . . . and ascend continually with absolute beauty as one's aim."[19] One must ascend beyond all particular beautiful states, and contemplate absolute beauty itself, "where it exists apart and alone."

19. Plato, *The Symposium* (trans. Hamilton), 94.

My problem is—and it may be seen by Thomists as an example of lamentable modernism—that I think that all beauties are particular states, and that "beauty" is an abstract term that covers many different types of thing, and has no objective existence. I do think that intrinsically worthwhile states are objective, in the sense that states are beautiful whether or not any human being thinks that they are. But they are all particular and very diverse states.

It makes sense to say such things as, "You ought to pursue beauty, truth, and goodness," the three transcendentals.[20] But I think one needs to spell this out as the endeavor to create and appreciate particular beautiful states, to achieve a correct and comprehensive understanding of the particular nature of things, and to be compassionate to and cooperative with others in many particular ways. Abstract terms like "beauty" are useful for classifying types of things and activities. But they do not refer to *entities*, which are, as Plato says, "apart from" particular beautiful states. They refer to what are largely dispositional states, denoting forms of activity aiming at general goals. Reference to transcendentals are therefore essentially hypothetical (if . . . then) statements, referring to forms of activity, not categorical statements referring to existent things. This means that they essentially include potentialities for forms of activity. If they are used to define perfection, then it is not true that the perfect being will be an existent "truth-itself," "beauty-itself," "goodness-itself," and "being-itself." On this understanding, in virtue of being absolutely perfect, God essentially has many unactualized potentialities. This is not a lack in God's being, but an essential property of a living and creatively acting God.

On this principle, which might be termed *the priority of the particular*, if one said that "God is perfect beauty," that would identify God with an abstract term that cannot refer to anything that objectively exists. The same would be true of any statement like, "God is perfect goodness" or "God is pure existence, *ipsum esse*"—the latter being precisely what Thomists are apt to say about God. From that, Thomists deduce that God, being pure existence, cannot have any unactualized potentialities. For a potentiality is something that could possibly be, but is not yet. Pure existence is pure actuality, and so excludes anything that is not actual. God is therefore the upper terminus of all positive abstract terms, all included in the most general term of all, "existence itself."

20. *Catechism of the Catholic Church*, section 41.

37

Fortunately, for those who doubt whether abstract nouns refer to entities, there is another way to construe such abstract statements. If pursuing perfect beauty is endeavoring to create and appreciate many beautiful states, then there could be a being that creates and appreciates the richest set of beautiful states, in terms of number (the greatest number of such states), diversity (the greatest variety of such states), and quality (the most beautiful of such states). There could be a being that generates *in itself* the greatest number, the greatest variety, and the greatest degree, of beautiful states. God's being will be of incomparable beauty, incomparable understanding, and incomparable beatitude. Such a being would not be simple. It would be extraordinarily complex. But it would conform to Anselm's definition of God as the most valuable being humans can conceive.

One could still say that it was simple, in the sense that it was like the simplicity of a conscious state, which may contain many complex features—for instance, many sights, sounds, and sensations—but they are bound together in *one indivisible consciousness*. They cannot be separated out as parts that combine to form a contingently connected whole.

Part of the concept of God's simplicity is the claim that all divine properties are identical with God's essence, and thus they are in fact identical with each other. The properties of wisdom and love seem to us to be different, but they refer to the same thing, the essence of God, which is identical with God's existence. The authors here appeal to Frege's distinction between sense and reference. "The morning star" and "the evening star" have different senses, but they refer to the same thing. However, this does not really help. There is no problem in saying that Venus can be clearly seen in the morning, and also, in a different place, in the evening. The star can be understood by everyone to be the same star. We know what a star (or a planet) is. But how can wisdom and love be identical? The same God can certainly be both wise and loving, but the divine ability to understand everything and the divine capacity to care for the well-being of others are different dispositional properties. No-one can see that it is obvious that wisdom and love are different expressions for the same property, or even really understand how they could be so. These are not just different descriptions for the same thing. We have no clear idea of what that "same thing" would be. It is just a dogmatic assertion that it must be the same thing if there cannot be different properties in God. But why could God not have different properties? They might all be inter-connected—God's understanding is strongly affected by God's care for others, and God's care for others requires an understanding of them. A qualified concept of simplicity might simply affirm that all divine properties are inextricably inter-connected, and are properties of the same personal being. But this is not the strong concept of simplicity that states that all divine properties are identical, and none of them involve dispositional features that would mean that being wise and loving entails acting in specifically wise and loving ways (which a personalist account would state). It is that strong concept that is at issue.

It is not true that, as one might (wrongly) suppose personalists think, God just happens to be the most beautiful thing around. God is the source of all beautiful states, and God sets the standard of beauty. Following the example of Plato's "Euthyphro Dilemma," one can ask whether things are beautiful because God says so (which seems to make beauty arbitrary), or whether God says things are beautiful because God accepts some independently existing standard of goodness (which makes God limited by some other and superior reality). Stump and Kretzmann suggest that the doctrine of divine simplicity resolves this dilemma by saying that God is goodness itself, the supreme form (*eidos*) or essence of beauty. This standard of beauty is thus internal to God, and we can say that God is "beauty itself."

I think they are right, except for the way they put it. There is a true definition of beauty, or a number of related definitions of different kinds of beauty. But that definition is not an existent universal, "beauty itself." Definitions, in general, do not refer to existing things. In the case of beauty, a definition would try to say what sorts of things are intrinsically worthwhile, worth creating and appreciating, for their own sake. There is probably not one definition that covers all sorts of beauty, and worthwhileness is a matter of what persons find happiness and fulfillment in contemplating. There are states that persons find intrinsically worthwhile, and that is so whether or not there is a God. But one could think of God as a conscious being who finds happiness and fulfillment in contemplating beautiful things.

As God is the greatest possible being, God has maximal knowledge, which is to know as true everything that is true. This includes knowledge of all possible worlds and states. Such knowledge is part of the mind of God. What is possible is not arbitrarily decided by God, and is not something other than God. It is what God knows, in knowing God's own mental contents. There is a truth about which possible states are supremely worth contemplating, and God, since God is maximally intelligent, inerrantly knows that truth. Knowledge of true beauty is internal to God. In contemplating God's own mind, God knows what is truly beautiful. Since God creates everything other than God, God will create in accordance with that knowledge, which is part of what God is.

This does not mean that God is "beauty itself." It means that God's self-knowledge defines, for all created beings, what beauty is, what things are truly beautiful. This resolves the Euthyphro Dilemma, not by saying that God is the pure form of beauty, but by saying that God, by knowing the divine nature, knows what things are beautiful, and also what things are good (what created persons ought to do, and have been created to do) and true (what the real nature of things is). On this alternative interpretation, God is not the pure form of anything. God is a mind that knows all possibles and actuals, and has the power to bring things into being for the sake of actualizing good and beautiful states.

This gives a positive reason for creation. There are some states of great beauty that can be actualized in a supreme personal being. They will be actualized contents of the divine consciousness. But there are many good and beautiful states that only finite persons can actualize. This includes every state that involves learning, developing, cooperating with others, and seeing things from a finite point of view. In other words, there are many values that can only be actualized by created persons. Most importantly, for Christians, compassionate love for those who are very different from oneself is such a value. If God shows compassionate *agape*, love, this can only be the case if there are other personal beings who are very different from God, who may even distance themselves from God as far as they can.

This, I think, brings us to the heart of the difference between a Thomist view of God and a more personalist view of God as a supreme and primordial mind or Spirit who creates in order to manifest the divine being in many creative, responsive, particular ways. If God is pure actuality, God can never do anything other than God does in a single eternal act, which is complete in itself without any creation. What are Thomists to do with the fact that God might not have created any world, that there are many possible worlds that God could have created, and that God created just this one, although, according to them, creating it makes no difference to God at all?

Stump and Kretzmann admit that the moves they make are counterintuitive. It looks as if, as far as common sense goes, God chooses between various possible worlds in order to actualize specific sorts of values, and the difference this makes to God is that such values are known and appreciated by God, which they would not have been if there had been no creation, or if there had been a different creation. Moreover, there are unactualized potentials in God if God creates any particular world, for God could have created (had the potential to create) a different world, but did not do so. Thus, the being of God is contingent and potential in some respects.

The authors resist this argument. They argue that this universe consists of "various temporal effects of the simple eternal act identical with God." But the problem is this: God is, *ex hypothesi*, simple and necessary. Thus, everything about God is necessarily what it is, including all God's causal acts and God's knowledge. This universe, however, is only one of many temporal universes, all or none of which God could create. If God is necessary, then the same God exists in all possible worlds (the authors accept this interpretation of necessity in section 7 of their article). And if those worlds are "effects" of God, then God is the cause of them. Thus, it might seem that the same God can cause many different, or no, universes. But if God is exactly the same in all possible worlds, and if all of God's causal acts are necessary, then necessarily God will cause the same universe in every possible world. More formally, if X is necessary and X causes Y, then nothing other than Y could be caused, and in that sense Y is necessary. In other words, no universe other than this is metaphysically (really) possible. This universe necessarily exists exactly as it does, and God necessarily creates it.

The distinction between logical possibility and real possibility is important to the authors. Logically, God could have done something other than God does (there are other non-contradictory possible worlds). But metaphysically, God being what God is in this world, it is not possible that God could create a different world. They say, "in any given initial-state set of worlds, God's act of will is one single metaphysically indivisible act."[21] I doubt that this really resolves the issue. It is saying that, given that God wills this world, God could not will a different world. But if God's will is necessary, God never could have willed a different world. Since worlds only exist by God's will, there are no other metaphysically possible worlds. Is this compatible with asserting the contingency of creation?

It is not conceivable, on this view, that there might be some events caused by God that are not necessarily what they are. Stump and Kretzmann argue that a wholly necessary God could create a contingent world, even a world containing libertarian freedom.[22] Then the creation of a world, and of

21. Kretzmann and Stump, "Absolute Simplicity," 373.
22. Kretzmann and Stump, "Absolute Simplicity," 373.

a specific world, would be necessary. But it might be possible that a necessary being could create a world to which there is no alternative, but that world may contain some contingent events. However, libertarian freedom requires that there is some initial state which has an effect that is not determined by anything that does not include the undetermined decision of an agent. If libertarian freedom exists, there are therefore events undetermined by God. If there are such events, God has to wait for a free decision to be made by a created agent, before God knows what happens next.[23] But God is changeless, and is not affected by anything that happens in the created world. Therefore, God cannot have some divine decisions dependent upon undetermined acts of creatures. That would require change in God, change from knowing that some acts are undetermined, for God has created them as such, to knowing what the agent has decided.

It is no use saying that since God's knowledge is eternal, God knows non-temporally what every agent decides. For God specifically creates some events as undetermined by God. Personal creatures can make different decisions, and this might lead to very large differences in the later effects of those decisions. As a result, God has to wait until some creatures determine them, before God carries on determining the rest of the world's history. Even if God's knowledge is non-temporal, it depends in part on what some creatures decide. So God is passible, affected by creation, and that means that what God knows before creation is different from what God knows after creation. God has changed. More formally put, if X knows Y and X is wholly necessary, then X's knowledge of Y is necessary (could not be otherwise). If X's knowledge of what is the case with Y could not be otherwise, then Y could not be otherwise, which is to say it could not be contingent, even in part.

If God determined everything in one eternal act of will, then nothing in the universe would be truly contingent, being one of many more or less equally possible states. Of course, one can have a compatibilist account of freedom, whereby freedom is compatible with complete determination. The authors do have such an account of freedom, derived from Aquinas. They say that freedom is having a natural inclination to good, plus an intellectual representation of what it good. More simply, freedom is just the

23. To consider the Molinist doctrine that God could eternally know even the results of libertarian free decisions would require a very long digression. I do say something about it later, but here I will just assume that if a decision really depends on a creature, that requires a certain passivity or receptivity in any other being who knows it.

rather negative fact of doing what one wants, and not being forced to do so by anyone or anything against one's will.

I think such an account is coherent, but leaves one with the belief that the existence of evil, of malice, and sheer stupidity, is brought about by God. Moral evil may be caused by refusal to will or by an intellectual mistake about what is good.[24] In either case, it is God who determines these things to be what they are. On the theory, God has no alternative. But why would a perfect God, who only wills good, do such things, and how could a perfect God punish people for what God has caused them to do?

The alternative, personalist, account is that God creates persons who have libertarian freedom. When God creates persons, God creates beings with their own causal power, who are "other" than God and who have an inner life of their own. Such persons do not, as Stump and Kretzmann think, just have happiness as their ultimate end, and do not just have an inclination to good. They also have inclinations to harm others, and they may discount happiness in favor of power or riches. That is their choice, and God will respond to such choices by punishing them (by depriving them of many goods and bringing them to feel and know the seriousness of their crimes), while always aiming at their ultimate well-being. Such a God is responsive and loving in ways that vary according to what creatures decide. It may be that God wills that everyone should ultimately accept and share in God's being as love. But even God cannot guarantee such a thing without undermining human freedom. So, God wills the welfare of all, but cannot ensure it. For Kretzmann and Stump that would be an unduly weak God, although the God some Christians, including perhaps Eleanor Stump, believe in, who has made sinners do what they do, will torture sinners forever in hell. The "weakness" of allowing created persons real freedom of self-determination may seem preferable to this.

Norman Kretzmann, in a later book[25] argues for the "Dionysian principle" that "Goodness is by its very nature diffusive of itself." While the word "diffusive" is not quite clear, he means that goodness naturally (I suppose that means necessarily) causes other good things to exist. Accordingly, he accepts that God's creation of a world is necessary (because it is caused by an act of God, which is necessarily what it is). This contradicts the statement

24. Kretzmann and Stump, "Absolute Simplicity," 365.
25. Kretzmann, *The Metaphysics of Theism*, 197.

[handwritten note: what various say about free will]

[handwritten note: free will is incompatible with causal determinism, against hr. free will]

43.

that "God's creating is not necessitated by the nature of deity"[26] and that God's will is "fully free as regards what to create."[27]

While I actually agree that God is fully free as regards what to create, such a claim threatens the simplicity of God, since some of God's acts (creating) will be necessary, and others (creating a particular universe) will be contingent. There are many possible good things, and God can only choose some of them to exist. However, this proposal entails that there are other things that God could create, but does not do so. These are unactualized potentialities in God, unless it is metaphysically impossible for God to create other than God does.

Again, the authors resist this conclusion. They put the case of a pharmacist who prescribes one medicine when he could prescribe many others that are just about equally good. They argue that this is not failing to actualize a potentiality. It is not a failure of any sort, and it does not impede the perfection of the pharmacist. In an analogous way, God choosing one world out of more or less equally good worlds is not a failure or a flaw in the divine perfection. That is true. But it is still the case that the pharmacist could have prescribed something different, but did not. There was something she could have done, but did not do. To say that she could have done it is to say that it was possible. To say that she did not do it is to say that she did not do what was possible. That is no failure, but it does entail that there are unactualized possibilities in her. In fact, the pharmacist analogy supports the view that God can choose between alternatives (is contingent in some respects), even though such choices show no lack in God, but rather illustrate an important aspect of divine perfection, the ability to make genuinely creative choices.

Given God has created X, it is no longer possible for God to create Y instead. Furthermore, since God is changeless there was no time in which God could have considered making a choice. Nevertheless, if God could have created Y, that is an unactualized possibility in God. The fact that it is not metaphysically possible, given that God has chosen X (that is, the "initial-state world" we are in), does not alter the fact that God might have, but did not, create Y. The only solution is to say that God could never have chosen other than God did, which is to say that there are not after all many possible worlds.

26. Kretzmann, *The Metaphysics of Theism*, 368.
27. Kretzmann, *The Metaphysics of Theism*, 224.

So, we are left with a totally necessary, totally determined, universe. How, then, can the authors hold that God could create a contingent universe (one that really could have been otherwise)? Perhaps God necessarily wills that some things are contingent (could have been otherwise)? But that has to be a purely logical, not a real, possibility.

There is another serious problem. If the existence of a universe is caused by the "diffusion of goodness," why is there so much evil in our world? Perhaps natural evils (earthquakes and storms) are a necessary part of any creation that could contain humans. There are, I think, good arguments from physics for that. But moral evil, the torture and enslaving of some humans by others, does not seem necessary. Yet, on the view, it too is necessarily caused by God. The defense that it is a necessary part of creation is possible. But it is hardly possible that it is necessary just because of the diffused goodness of God. If God the creator is wholly necessary, God is not perfectly good, but a sort of mixture of morally neutral or even destructive necessity and the will to cause goodness. I actually think this is quite a good explanation. But it looks like a complication of any view that God is simple, and that every divine property is identical to every other. The property of causing destructive evil is not identical to the property of causing good states. It seems to imply a difference between what necessarily issues from God, and what God (also necessarily) intentionally wills.

The situation seems worse when one comes to the Johannine statement that "the Word became flesh" (John 1:14). For necessitarians, the incarnation is unavoidable, and the passion of Jesus does not affect the divine nature in any way. But if, in Christ, the humanity of Jesus is united to the divine nature to form "one person," it seems hard to say that the divine nature having united human nature to itself is no different from the divine nature considered alone. This would be a strange form of unity, which makes it impossible to say that God in person walked among us or died for us. It was Jesus who did that, and though Jesus is "one" with the divine nature, what he did was not done by the divine nature. This seems like a strong form of dualism, though it is meant to preserve the truth of the incarnation of God in human history. A personalist account would say that if two different natures are united in one compound unity (a "person," in traditional terms), then each one, while remaining itself, would be affected by the other.

The doctrine of *communicatio idiomatum* holds that, because two natures are united, what you can say about one nature you can say about the other. But that is just a remark about what you can say, a rule of grammar. It does not mean that each nature *in fact* shares any properties with the other, or is affected in any way by the other. But I think that means that there is no real unity between the natures.

A similar problem arises with the doctrine of *theosis*, the view that all creation is to participate in the divine nature (2 Pet 1:4), and is to be assumed into God. If humans are to be truly "in" God, then God is surely changed by that inclusion. "God is Spirit" (John 4:24), and Supreme Spirit creates many persons who are other than God, but whose destiny is that they should relate to God so closely that, to use the biblical analogy of marriage as "one flesh" (Gen 2:24), they become one. That, I think, is what it means for all creation to be united in Christ, which for me is a central hope of Christian faith.

On a personalist account of God, God is not a being who happens to instantiate in itself all perfections in their maximal form. Rather, God is that which is *necessary* in existence, in supreme knowing, in maximal wisdom, power, beauty, and goodness. God does not just "will his own goodness," God is *essentially and necessarily* good.[28] God wills a limitless number of particular intrinsically good states, prominent among which are the creative and responsive relationships among contingent persons and between them and the uniquely all-creating Spirit. God is a creator with unlimited potency, a necessarily existing mind that generates a limitless variety of goods that could not all exist just in God alone.

IMPASSIBILITY?

Divine Passion

Thomas Weinandy holds that "God is passionate in love, mercy, and compassion."[29] This is indeed central to a Christian account of God. But if God is changeless and impassible, God cannot be in two or more successive states, and God cannot be changed by anything that happens in creation, unless God has eternally decreed that it should happen, so that this is not a case of God being changed by something other than God or what God has unilaterally decreed. If divine love was something like the appreciative contemplation of unchanging beauty, then it would not imply any change of state in God—that is probably Plato's notion of love of the good and

28. Kretzmann and Stump, "Absolute Simplicity," 365.

29. Weinandy, *Does God Suffer?* 37.

46

beautiful, an idea repeated and developed by Aristotle in his account of God in *Metaphysics lambda*. But suppose that there are different sorts and degrees of beauty, as there are in creation. It seems that divine contemplation would have a different affective mood, ranging from appreciation to distaste, depending on the sort and degree of beauty that was contemplated.

Love, even love of unchanging beauty, is not simply cognition. It carries with it an affective component. Loving implies finding happiness in knowing something. Or, if the object contemplated is not beautiful or good, love implies something like pity or desire that it should be better. Thus, love of a creature implies both finding happiness in its well-being and relative unhappiness in its imperfection.

Love is also a motivating factor. It is not enough that a loving being should feel unhappy at my suffering. If it is really loving, desiring my good, it will do something about it. The Christian idea of love as *agape*, found in 1 John 4:8, implies an active element: "God so loved the world that he *gave* his only Son" (John 3:16). Concern for the well-being of creatures implies knowledge of their condition, pity if it involves suffering, revulsion if it involves the willful causing of suffering, and action to relieve that suffering where it is possible.

There may be, as Dr. Weinandy is concerned to emphasize, a changeless disposition in God to help creatures to achieve well-being. But the simple contemplation of creaturely suffering, even if coupled with pity for their condition, is not truly love. The one who truly loves will do something to help. This entails both possibility—the existence of an affective state that is caused by knowledge of creatures—and successivity, for example, the existence of a state of pity with regard to sorrow, followed by action and then a state of satisfaction when the action is successful.

God's changeless disposition to be merciful also implies a knowledge that some creaturely act deserving judgment has actually occurred, which knowledge could only exist if there is, and because there is, creation. This is a case where some divine knowledge is dependent upon something other than God. Even if God necessarily creates the world, the actual existence of a world causes God to feel and act differently than God would have acted without creation. It could be said that God is responding to God's own act in creation. This is not responding to something completely other than, and independent of, God. Nevertheless, it entails that God's affective nature is dependent in some ways upon God's creating a world, and upon the precise nature of the world that God creates. Unlike Aristotle's God, this God knows the world and responds to it in appropriate ways. Moreover, being merciful entails responding to actions of which God disapproves, which reinforces the point that God does not positively desire everything in creation to exist exactly as it does. This implies a response in God that could only exist if creatures other than God actually exist, and if God does not positively desire that they should exist exactly as they do.

It seems, then, that it only makes sense to say that God is passionately loving and merciful if God is *affected by creation* (not necessarily changed by, if his decrees to create were eternal) and acts in specific ways within creation (like raising Jesus from death). God will act in specific ways because of the nature of the world that God creates. I think that what Dr. Weinandy fears is that this will make God dependent on something other than God, which undermines divine sovereignty, and that it is too anthropomorphic a view of God to make God a causal agent in the world. He says, "To make God passible . . . undercuts the wholly otherness of God."[30]

I share with him a concern to preserve the self-existence and transcendence of God, but, as I have suggested, I do not think that the expression "wholly other" is very helpful. If it means "other in every respect," then nothing in all creation is anything like God. How, then, could humans be made in God's image, or how could Jesus be "the visible image of the invisible God" (Col 1:15)? If we can truly say that God is love or wisdom (*Sophia*) or Spirit, these words must be appropriate for us to use. Even if we cannot thereby pretend to know just what God is like, at least we know that God is more like these things than God is like hatred or stupidity or like a material object.

So, God is a causal agent which is active in the world, though God is not like a created cause which operates according to general laws, or even like a personal created cause which pursues goals that may be unwise or immoral. God's purposes are always wise and good, but their implementation involves a divine responsiveness to the actions of creatures if God is to be truly loving. That does not undermine God's sovereignty, because it is solely God who decrees that there should be a creation, and solely God who wills that creation should affect the divine both affectively and cognitively. Moreover, this is just a small part of God's knowledge and God's being, which leaves the necessary aspects of the divine nature untouched.

---

30. Weinandy, *Does God Suffer?* 63.

Divine Knowledge of Creaturely Feelings

To say that God is passible is to say that God is affected by the beauties and sufferings of the created world. I have held that if God truly knows what is actual in creation, this knowledge will involve an affective component. It will include knowing what it is like to be a conscious being in the world. This means that the beauty of eternal bliss is qualified by the knowledge and feeling of the suffering of creatures. God, as omniscient, knows what it is like for a creature to suffer. For instance, if a creature is depressed, God is not depressed, but God will know what it is like for a creature to be depressed. "Knowing what it is like" is more than a purely conceptual knowledge that something is the case. It is being able to share a creature's way of seeing things or feelings. If God truly knows the secrets of all hearts, then God will in some way include all the feelings of human hearts in the divine consciousness.

There are clearly problems about this, problems that are brought out very well in Richard Creel's book *Divine Impassibility*. He holds that God cannot change in the divine nature, the divine will, the divine feelings, or the divine knowledge of all possibilities. Any change in these respects would be incompatible with the divine perfection, which excludes the possibility of divine change, indecision, or suffering in God. He is particularly scathing about those who believe that reality would be better if God suffered or changed his mind, arguing that such things would be imperfections. Yet his position is more complex than it may seem. He also holds that God is passible in two respects, in knowledge of what is temporally actual ("A changing thing can be known as changing only by a knower whose awareness follows along with it")[31] and knowledge of the future free actions of finite persons ("the future free actions of creatures are something that in principle cannot be known").[32]

He thereby seems committed to a view of God as impassible in some respects and passible in others. The lines between these two aspects do not quite fall where he draws them, that is, between knowledge of actualities on the one hand and the divine nature, will, and feeling, on the other. It is possible that God may know all possible states, and may eternally decide, or pre-determine, the divine response to all of these states; that is what Creel means by saying that God is impassible in will. Yet if God does not

31. Creel, *Divine Impassibility*, 88.
32. Creel, *Divine Impassibility*, 206.

know the future free actions of creatures, then God cannot know which of the divine predetermined responses will be actualized. And since in Creel's opinion God's knowledge of what is actual can only be known when it becomes actual, God will know the actual divine response to human free actions only in response to, and when, such human decisions are made. The divine responses will not be wholly determined by God, but are partly determined by the free decisions of creatures. This is a clear case of the passibility of the divine will.

Furthermore, the divine will (what God decides to do) is part of the divine nature. That is, if God ever acts contingently (in response to human decisions that could have been otherwise), then it must be part of the nature of God that God is able to act contingently. Such contingency will depend in part on what free creatures decide. Therefore, part of God's nature is passible—it is capable of being affected by what beings other than God do.

That means that the dual nature of God, as envisaged by Creel, must be ascribed to divine nature and will, as well as to divine knowledge of what becomes actual in the created world. Must it also be the case with what God feels, so that God is at least partly passible in feelings?

Creel does not hesitate to ascribe feeling to God. He accepts that God is beatifically happy in contemplation of the divine perfections, and happiness is a feeling state. But he denies that God's feeling state is affected by what happens in the world, and in particular by the existence of pain, suffering, and such feelings as hatred and anger, which exist in created persons. Yet again he is rather equivocal about this. He says that "God knows himself as eternally blissful, and as knowing the pain . . . , etc. of the other,"[33] where knowledge of the pain of another is a sort of telepathic awareness of what it is like for another to feel pain.

Such telepathic knowledge, however, would not exist if there were no creatures actually feeling pain, and it is a response to contingent events, since the world might not even have existed. God feels bliss as a result of knowing the divine nature, presumably as something intrinsically worthwhile, to be valued and cherished. God also knows some actual things, such as pain and greed in some creatures, which are not worthwhile, and are to be eschewed and eliminated if possible. This contingent knowledge cannot cause bliss. Are we to suppose, then, that it causes no appropriate feeling state at all in the God who knows every possible thing?

33. Creel, *Divine Impassibility*, 132.

It certainly, for Creel, produces appropriate actions, of seeking to defeat pain and hatred. God not only knows that such things as pain and hatred exist. God thinks that it is bad that they exist, that they should not exist or should be defeated. God does not feel neutral about them, as a being with no feelings but only pure cognition would (if there is such a possible being). One can only suppose that God would feel unhappiness about them (i.e., a dislike of them and a feeling that they should not exist).

I would expect believers in God to think that such things as pain and anger are ineliminable, in the sense they are necessary possibilities of a world like this, and they have been regrettably been actualized. But they can in future be eliminated and defeated by divine and human actions, and they will be so defeated at the end of this historical age. We might say that God is unhappy about them, but accepts that their present existence was unpreventable, given the nature of this world and the ways in which the freedom of creatures has been exercised, and knows that they will certainly be defeated, leaving a world of immense value and bliss, which would otherwise not have existed.

Creel emphasizes these points, that God sees the wrongful use of freedom as unpreventable, and that God will bring all things to an overwhelmingly good conclusion. He rightly says that this will make a difference to how God feels about pain and hatred. But is he right in saying that God's feeling state will nevertheless be unchangeably one of perfect bliss, despite the wrongs that humans do, and the pains they suffer? Thinking of the doctrine of hell, he writes that even "If we choose against his Kingdom, he will not be distraught."[34] God may not be *distraught* at the knowledge that there are people in hell, but it seems insensitive to say that God will be blissful in the presence of their sufferings, even if they deserve them. Such a thought seems to imply that God knows and regards only the divine state itself, and not the affective states of the beings God has created. However, if God's knowledge is responsive to what is actual in the world (as Creel allows), and if God feels bliss as a result of knowing the divine nature, it seems that God will feel appropriately in God's responsive knowledge of events in the world. The appropriate feeling will, in many cases, be one of approval and appreciation, as God knows the many beautiful and good things that happen. But in other cases, like those manifesting anger or pain, the appropriate feeling would be one of disapproval or compassion, respectively. In the case of hell, either all will be liberated from it, so that God's attitude would

34. Creel, *Divine Impassibility*, 141.

change from one of condemnation and disapproval to one of acceptance and approval, which could indeed be overwhelmingly good. Or, if hell is everlasting (which it is hard to see as compatible with God's goodness), God's attitude would at best be described as one of satisfied justice, not bliss in contemplating something beautiful and good.

Creel is probably right in saying we should not attribute pain or anger to God. But he is almost certainly wrong in saying that "if God's suffering is eternally overwhelmed, transformed, or transcended by his joyful essence or knowledge, then he never suffers."[35] Transformed suffering is still suffering, though the character of that suffering is modified by the knowledge that it will be transformed. Perhaps it would be better not to call it suffering, in God's case, since God will not be consumed or destroyed by it, as humans can be. The appropriate attitude to human depravity might not be a bout of fierce divine anger. But it will certainly not be one of contemplative bliss, and it will not be one of total indifference. It will be one of disapproval and discontent, allied with a disposition to act in order to change the offending object of knowledge. God's feelings are not our feelings; but if God has knowledge that is more than purely intellectual, God will have feelings of compassion and condemnation. God will be passible and passionate—even though it will be true to say that God's love and concern for the good even of the depraved will never change.

Creel suggests at one point that "it is in principle impossible for any being to know directly the subjectivity of another."[36] All experiences are private and incommunicable, as experiences. This principle would effectively rule out any possibility of God knowing directly any human experiences. Since such experiences (what it feels like to sense something from my point of view) undoubtedly exist, there would be lots of things in existence that God could not know directly. I therefore feel inclined to say that telepathy is possible, and Creel seems to accept this, calling it "indirect knowledge." One person could in principle experience what it is like for another person to feel as they do. In such a case, the person would be aware that the experiences were experiences of another person, and would not regard them as experiences of her own.

As such, the telepathically known experiences would co-exist with a set of the telepath's personal attitudes towards them. Pleasant and worthwhile experiences would evoke feelings of joy or approbation. Painful or

35. Creel, *Divine Impassibility*, 134.

36. Creel, *Divine Impassibility*, 129.

worthless experiences might evoke feelings of pity or revulsion. Thus, the telepath would not feel the known experiences in the same way as the primary experient did.

Such experiences would be taken into the divine consciousness, but not as God's own experiences. They would co-exist with divine responsive attitudes of joy, pity, or disapproval. When Creel says that "God can know our pain and pleasure . . . without thereby having these experiences as his own,"[37] he is correct. Yet God cannot really be said to know our pain and pleasure without having these experiences added to the divine consciousness in some form.

We might thus suppose that God would wish to attend to and enjoy worthwhile human experiences; empathize with experiences of pain and suffering, while understanding their transience and the part they play in the wider context of created being; and condemn ("hate" is the biblical word; in Hebrew, *sānē'* or *za'ap*, and a range of similar terms) evil thoughts and desires, consigning them to eternal forgetfullness and disregard.

A perfect being would, I think, feel sadness for the frustration of the divine purposes. If not anger, then at least revulsion or distaste. God will continue, one supposes, to care for the good even of those who are evil. But achieving that good will require a change in their character, repentance and a "new birth."

The question will then be, what is the most effective way to bring this about? It would need to be shown that God still cares for evil persons, and wishes them to be fulfilled in goodness, and is able to bring that about. Yet God condemns what they are doing, and the evil must be eliminated or compensated for (atoned for) in some way.

This is a dual feeling of concern to bring out a core of goodness in the wrongdoer, and correction of the evil that has been done, and of the motivations and desires that the wrongdoer has.

Much evil cannot be compensated for—nothing can undo or compensate for murder or genocide. All that can change is the desires of the wrongdoer and some genuine effort on the wrongdoer's part to accept some penalty and help to avoid murders in general, perhaps. That is to say, some form of penance aimed at reformation is required.

What can turn the human heart? Seeing the desolation that follows from evil, and seeing that there is an indestructible love that endures all evil, perhaps. For Christians, it is the cross that shows the terrible desolation

---

37. Creel, *Divine Impassibility*, 130.

that evil causes; and it also shows the indestructible love that calls for a breaking and renewing of the heart.

God's affective attitude to evil will be one of revulsion and sadness. But that sounds rather passive, and indeed there is a passive element in the divine knowledge of creation. Divine beatitude may be overwhelming, but it is modified by revulsion and sadness. Those elements do not remain passive, however. They engender action intended to bring about penance and reformation. This action will express the resolve to destroy evil and effect union with goodness. Revulsion and sadness are "moments" in the divine life, and they are always allied with positive endeavors to realize goodness, with hope for newness of life. They are also allied with the certainty of universal bliss for all who respond to the divine invitation. Forgiveness is not simply remission of penalty; it is faith in the inner goodness of creatures, the call for them to realize goodness and the promise of its real possibility. The history of the universe might well appear to be the history of a journey "from infinite sorrow to infinite joy" (an expression used by Hegel, in his *Lectures on the Philosophy of Religion*).

Richard Creel argues that there is no moral obligation on God to feel the sorrows of creatures.[38] That is true; but if God's nature is love, concern for the good of creatures, God will naturally do all God can to make their good possible. That does, I think, entail that God will understand and empathize with their sorrow, and that God knows what it is like for beings to be sorrowful, as well as what it is like for beings to be vindictive and destructive.

"Knowing what it is like" is not being the thing that one knows (e.g., knowing what it is like to be depressed is not actually being depressed). Nor is it a feelingless registration that depression exists. It is total empathy or fellow-feeling, held within a totality of millions of other different feelings, and within the fundamental bliss of the eternal being.

It is not enough that God feels suffering in one human case, the case of Jesus, however intense that suffering is. One human experience cannot possibly contain every sort of human feeling. Even Jesus can only experience what is possible for a man of his time and place—he cannot, for instance, feel what it is to be a woman or an old man with Alzheimer's. What Jesus manifests and expresses is what God is eternally like. Thus, Jesus expresses in one human case the truth that God empathizes with every creaturely feeling at all times and places. Empathy cannot mean concurrence or

38. Creel, *Divine Impassibility*, 147.

agreement, for as well as knowing what human suffering is like, God also knows what it is like for a creature to be evil and depraved. This is a feeling that is alien to God's nature. It is as if a father empathizes with the hatred his son feels, but at the same time condemns that feeling, and seeks to change it. God understands it and why and how it arises, but does not accept it as God's own. For Christians, only in the case of Jesus can God accept all the feelings of a human person as God's own. There is a difference between human hatred and divine knowledge of the feeling of hatred. Sympathy does not seem quite the right word for this. It is a form of "affective understanding," and it arouses in God "anger" and "sorrow." It is a mixture of complete understanding combined with judgment, and the will to heal or reform. This sort of love is both modified by what happens in creation, and actively seeks to change human hearts by actions that are redemptive, that have the power to show that evil ends in death, and yet that love can eliminate evil, take broken human hearts and bring them to new (eternal) life.

On this account, it is not quite true to say that God suffers. God is not damaged or destroyed by divine knowledge of the suffering of creatures. As Rowan Williams says, "If there is 'emotion' of some sort in the Word, it cannot be identical with what I as a finite subject feel."[39] Dr. Williams goes on to conclude that this would make the Word "another member of a class of knowing subjects," which is impossible. However, I feel inclined to say that God is a member of a class of knowing subjects—God knows many things. God is not, of course, a member of a class of finite knowing subjects. But God feels anger, pity, sorrow, compassion, and sympathy, which would not exist without creatures. And God "knows the secrets of the heart" (Ps 44:21), which implies that God has access to the innermost desires and thoughts of creatures, even when they are not expressed. So, God knows what it is like to suffer, and also what it is like to torture and kill others, and what it is like to be estranged from God. In a word, God knows tragedy, not just unchanging and pure bliss.

The cross manifests this property of God in a human life. It shows that this is not just a passive knowledge or sharing of experience. It evokes an active response in God of judging and healing, of anger and compassion. What is "other"—the suffering and sin of creatures—enters into God, evoking an affective response of compassion and judgment, together with a concern to bring creatures to union with the divine nature in the most appropriate ways.

39. Williams, *Christ the Heart of Creation*, 20.

Dr. Weinandy, like Richard Creel, asks what good it would be for God to suffer—he suggests that would only add one more case of suffering to reality, which is not good. As I have suggested, God does not suffer as creatures do, though God is affectively influenced by the sufferings, and joys, of creatures. The question is not, however, whether divine suffering does good. The question is about the nature of divine knowledge. Few theists would deny that God knows what is the case. Is this some sort of purely intellectual knowledge, knowledge without any feeling component? If so, could it be said that God knows what it is like to be a creature? If God is love, this is a total self-giving and a sharing of being with another. Knowledge of the inner lives of creatures has to be a sort of sharing in their lives. The other will remain other, but knowledge of others will affect the knower. In fact, God will presumably know the inner lives of creatures better than they know themselves. This will move God to empathetic understanding, and such understanding will generate a feeling response, whether of repulsion or compassion or pleasure. God's affective knowing has two components lacking in purely intellectual knowledge—empathetic understanding of what it is like to be a creature, and empathetic response that seeks to find for creatures a way of liberation from despair and a reorientation of their lives towards goodness.

It is not irrational, indeed it seems wholly appropriate, that such a divine response should take the form of a manifestation of divine life in a human life, a presentation in that life of the nature of true goodness, a dramatic revelation of the suffering and death that is the consequence of human selfishness and greed, often the suffering of the innocent, though in the long run the suffering of the evil-hearted too. It is also a disclosure of God's uniquely affective knowledge of all the sufferings and joys of humanity, and a demonstration of the power of love to meet and overcome those sufferings and the evils associated with them.

IMMUTABILITY?

On many early Christian accounts of God, there is another philosophical dogma at work, and though this would follow from the doctrines of absolute simplicity and of impassibility, it might be held independently. It is that the changeless is superior to the changing, so the Supreme Being must be changeless. This is very difficult to square with the biblical record. Consider the conversation between God and Moses in Exodus 32:7-14. God threatens to destroy the people who have worshipped the golden calf. But Moses pleads with God, and "the Lord changed his mind about the disaster that he planned to bring on this people." There are many other occasions when God is said to change his mind, and they all raise problems about saying that God is changeless. This is the point at which the biblical view decisively differs from a Platonic conception of the timeless good, which never reacts to humans in a personal, much less a conversational, way.

One possible view is that this record of a conversation between God and Moses is an extended metaphor. It never literally took place. It is a story that shows that God's justice demands punishment, but that God's mercy will always triumph to give people another chance. Or perhaps it took place, but God did not really change his mind. God was warning that justice was appropriate, but testing Moses' faith, and finally assuring Moses of divine mercy. It was Moses who feared divine judgment and pleaded successfully for mercy. God remained changeless throughout.

This is a possible explanation. But it is very misleading to speak of a changeless being as though it could be influenced by human prayers. In the absence of very strong reasons for ascribing changelessness to God, it looks as though the Bible is suggesting that God can be influenced by human prayers and actions.

As we have seen, for Aquinas, Moses' prayer and God's response are not new and unforeseen acts. They are acts that are part of the one complete creation of the whole of space and time in one non-temporal act. All of Moses' words and God's words were caused in that same non-temporal act. They have to be, because God is not in time and does not change in response to what Moses says. So, one has a completely determined creation, in which all things without exception, from the beginning to the end of time, are decreed by God's changeless will.

It should be noted that this view is neither metaphorically nor analogically true. It is just literally true (or, of course, false). The universe exists because of one all-determining intentional act. The Bible never says this, but then the Bible rarely says anything quite so philosophical. How, then, are we to assess its truth?

One consideration is that it seems unduly misleading for the Bible to say that God speaks, Moses prays, and God changes his mind, when the truth is that God has from all eternity decreed that Moses will pray as he does, and that God will then seem to change his mind. For in fact God has not changed his mind. God has always known that he will pardon the

57

people, so was it not a pretense that he would destroy them? It is as if God said, "I am going to threaten destruction; but I am going to ensure that you ask for mercy, and I will then be merciful." It seems more straightforward to say, "I will destroy them unless you ask for mercy, and that is up to you." This would entail that there is more than one possible future, and which one occurs really depends in part upon what some human does. God lets the future depend, in some respects, on what humans themselves decide. God remains in control, because God sets the limits of human freedom, and may well exercise an influence that will help people to make the right choices, though they may be too weak on their own to put them fully into effect.

In favor of the first option, it preserves God's absolute sovereignty and power over creation. In favor of the second, it gives humans a degree of real freedom and responsibility for what happens in part of creation. It enables God not to be a total controller, but rather to be an enabler and persuader who has the good of the universe at heart, but wants creatures to realize unique goods by their own efforts.

THE EXISTENCE OF EVIL

The decisive factor, as I noted when discussing Stump and Kretzmann, is the existence of great suffering and evil in creation. There is no way in which a good God could desire the existence of such things for their own sakes. They must in some way be unavoidable in the sort of creation God chooses.

If God is totally necessary in the choices God makes and in the sort of being God is, one might just say that suffering and evil are necessary, and that is that. But the Bible speaks of a war between good and evil, between God and Satan. The Book of Revelation states that "war broke out in heaven" (Rev 12:7). Though God was, unsurprisingly, victorious, it is clear that God and his forces actively oppose Satan and his angels. Isaiah also speaks of a long struggle between Leviathan and God, which is to end with God slaying the monstrous beast (Isa 27:1).

This image rather obviously derives from the Babylonian creation-myth of the primeval war between Marduk, the god of Babylon, and Tiamat, the salt-sea monster of chaos, but it has been woven into a mono-theistic account of creation. There is now one creator of all things, so in some way chaos itself must be part of created reality, yet it must be a power

58

just speculation, logical speculation, anthromorphic

forces of evil

that strives against or resists the creator's plans, and will inevitably be defeated, though only after a long struggle. The Hebrew Bible does not resolve questions about the ultimate origin of or reason for the existence of evil and chaos. But it does seem that God does not actually *desire* and consciously *intend* the existence of such things. Rather, God seeks to limit or eliminate them. For example, even if God creates Satan, God subsequently fights against and overcomes Satan, which entails that God does not intend that Satan should rebel, though God makes it possible for it to happen. This in turn entails that some things exist and are created that God does not will, and indeed opposes. That is, God is not in total control, but is limited in some way by opposing forces of evil. That in turn decreases the attraction of saying that God is changeless, since the biblical view speaks of a struggle between good and evil, and of the final elimination of evil. These things entail change from struggle to victory.

Suffering, evil, and chaos must somehow spring from God, since there is nothing else they could spring from, in a biblical view of God. But how can things spring from God that God does not desire, and that God opposes? A tempting suggestion is that they are just necessary. God, supreme Spirit, has a "dark side," which is destined to be overcome through a long cosmic war. It is also possible to say that much suffering originates in, or that the degree of suffering is immeasurably increased by, the moral freedom of creatures, angelic or human, to reject the wisdom and love of God. And it is possible to say that God creates an autonomous universe of creatures, which must slowly develop through effort and disciple to become vehicles of Spirit. This makes possible the virtues of creative endeavor and compassionate relationship. But it also makes possible the vices of destructive competition, greed, and hatred. Then evil is a natural, if not inevitable, possibility of a significantly autonomous creation.[40]

These possibilities differ, but they are closely connected. For the possibilities of evil must lie, if only as possibilities, in the being of God. Many of them could well be inseparably bound up with the possibilities of goodness that God positively wills and intends. Some of these negative possibilities are realized, or intensified, by creaturely choices of self-will. And self-will is rooted in creaturely alignment with or indifference to the creative purposes inherent in a developing universe.

---

40. I set out this view more fully, under the heading of "the principle of plenitude," in *Religion and the Modern World*, ch. 13.

The biblical view is not an evolutionary view, in anything like a modern sense. But it does have a view of human history as one of a "fall," or an increasing succession of falls, from the ideals that underlie divine creation, of a long struggle between good and evil, and of a final triumph of good and the elimination of evil. These things are depicted in the highly symbolic forms of apocalyptic thought, and they imply a changing involvement of God in the initial creation (the "six days" of increasingly complex life), in the subsequent struggle between good and evil (the "war in heaven"), and in the final victory of good (the descent of the New Jerusalem together with hosts of angels from the sky).

If God creates an autonomous and developing universe, then God gives some causal control to creatures. If the choices that intelligent creatures make are truly autonomous, then they involve an element of contingency. They often could be otherwise than they are. Humans choose evil, but they could have chosen good. God did not make them choose evil. Indeed, God commanded them not to choose evil, and punished them (according to the biblical record) for making a choice God did not want them to make.

This does not deprive God of control and authority. It just means that this is the sort of universe that God creates, one that has a limited set of alternative futures that are ultimately under the control of God, but that God allows to follow in particular cases from the actions of creatures.

In short, creation changes God; if the universe exists, something is true of God that might not have been true. God knows that many contingent events actually occur, and their occurrence is not solely due to God's actions. God's knowledge partly depends on events that are other than God. God is changed by something other than God, though not by anything that is completely independent of God. Creatures would not exist without God, yet God depends in part (for some of God's knowledge) on what creatures freely do.

Moreover, free creaturely acts largely determine much of what will happen subsequently. If God is to control the universe at all, God will have to take account of these contingent changes in planning the ongoing future of the cosmos. In other words, God will need to respond to creaturely acts by taking account of them in continuing the cosmos on in time. This introduces a great deal of contingency in God, and much responsiveness to temporal events in God's continuing creation of the cosmos.

To make this view coherent, we have to suppose that God is necessary in some respects (necessary in existence and in the divine nature as wise and loving), but contingent in others (in divine knowledge of freely chosen creaturely actions). Aquinas utilized such a double-aspect concept when he said, for example, that "angels combine unchangeable existence with changeability of choice at the natural level, and with changeability of thoughts, affections."[41] Angels, Aquinas thought, are unchangeable in respect of existence, but changeable in respect of their thoughts and affections.

The idea of divine simplicity might be thought to rule out the view that God is necessary in some respects and contingent in others. But if divine simplicity is construed as I have done, as affirming an indivisible unity of diverse properties, it is perfectly coherent to say that necessary and contingent properties of God are indivisibly united in the divine nature. Perhaps it is even necessarily true that God has some contingent properties, and necessarily true that they will be exercised in some specific ways.

Overall, I conclude that a general biblical account of God is more sympathetic to the view that God changes in some respects than to the view that God is completely changeless. This is supported by the philosophical consideration that any being that was not temporal at all would be incapable of framing new purposes, of responding to creatures, or of doing creatively new things. There are a huge number of things—in fact, all genuinely temporal things—it would be logically unable to do. That hardly seems an adequate idea of a God who is "almighty."

It goes without saying that God is not temporal in the sense of being part of our space-time. But if time is, as Aristotle said, the measure of change, then any sort of non-spatial change in God is a form of temporality. The Einsteinian point that space and time are inseparable in our universe, would not hold for any being that was not physical or spatial. Change in God is primarily spiritual or mental change. There can be a sort of successiveness in the knowledge and actions of God, and this makes it appropriate to speak of God as a creative mind responsive to the cosmos.

We might not want to say that God thinks in the same way a finite person thinks, but we would not want to say that "God thinks" is false in its primary sense, as it would be if it were a metaphor. God is conscious of what God is doing, and brings events about for a reason, or with some purpose. However hard it is to imagine how God thinks or intends, and however different God's thoughts and intentions are from human thoughts

41. Aquinas, *Summa Theologiae*, 1a, 10, 5.

and intentions, it is just true (or, of course, just false) that God is conscious of possible states of affairs, and intends to bring them about. So however analogical "God creates" may be, it entails some straightforwardly true statements, such as "God consciously and intentionally brings about some states of affairs." And it entails the denial of some literally true statements, such as "God does not know what God is doing," and "God did not intend to create the world." Being conscious and intentional, God is in some sense a mind, more like a conscious intelligent mind than God is like anything else that we can imagine in this universe.

GOD'S ACTS IN THE WORLD

As a conscious mind with a purpose for creation, it is reasonable to think that God intends to bring about some created states that will serve as communications or appearances of God. If we try to think of God as God is in Godself, apart from creation, that will obviously involve no such created appearances. Thus, in creating a universe within which God appears, God performs acts that God would not have performed if there was no creation. Thinking of God as an uncreated mind, we can say that the mind of God can create a universe, and also create appearances that are able to communicate with embodied and created human minds. According to a straightforward reading of the Hebrew Bible, God causes some particular events that often or even usually have a more than ordinary scientific explanation (like the burning bush) to become symbolic expressions of the divine transcendent nature.

Do these appearances show what God truly is? "God is Spirit" (John 4:24). God is not flesh, is not part of the physical universe, and has no physical brain or body. God in the divine being itself contains no physical component. Therefore, any physical appearances of God cannot depict what God *in se* actually is. Yet it is truly God who uses physical appearances to convey something true about the divine nature or will. It follows that these appearances do not by any means convey the full and essential nature of God. They may convey the thought that God is a being of great majesty, power, and loving-kindness, and this thought is true. But they do not "show what God is," for the simple reason that God has no physical form.

It follows that God is a causal factor in producing such theophanies, and that God can correctly be described as the one who speaks and appears, and does so in finite forms, which are as such incapable of conveying the fullness of the divine glory, though something true about God is conveyed. In other words, God is a member of the set of non-physical entities that speak and appear; a cause who makes things happen in the world that would not otherwise have happened; and one who acts in ways in which God would not have been able to act if there had been no world in existence.

In saying this, one is by no means denying that God far exceeds full human comprehension. God's causality is not bound by physical processes, as most causal factors in the world are. And it may well be that God is the only member of the set of non-natural entities that speak and appear to humans. More probably, I think, there may be many such entities (many "gods," even if such entities are possible rather than actual), but God, the God of Abraham and Isaac, is the only such entity that is the creator of everything but itself, and so in fact is the only God in a more fully defined sense.

There is very little in all this to suggest that God is "wholly other" or "wholly beyond comprehension." Those are not biblical terms, though the Bible is at pains to point out that God's thoughts (which entails that God does have thoughts) are not like human thoughts, and that God can never be adequately understood by men or angels. It rather seems that God is like humans in many ways, and especially in having consciousness, thoughts and purposes. Yet God is unlike humans in the way God possesses these attributes. That, I take it, is what Aquinas means to say when he says that we can make true, though analogical, statements about God. Unfortunately, as I have argued, Aquinas also says things that threaten to deprive such analogical statements of meaning. The main problems here are the Thomist doctrines of divine simplicity and changelessness. Neither of these doctrines can be found in the Bible. They are purely philosophical ideas, though of course they are none the worse for that. As I have indicated, both are capable of a helpful interpretation—namely, that God contains all compossible perfections in indivisible unity, and that God is unchangeable in existence, in supreme wisdom, power, and love. But if taken in a very strong sense, they undermine the meaning of statements about God thinking and deciding. For then they entail that God cannot have new creative thoughts and cannot decide to do anything that God has not eternally decreed. These I take to be grievous limitations on the perfection of God.

My conclusion is that, while there is not one systematic and unchanging idea of God in the Bible, yet the most fully developed idea of God in the major prophets certainly sees God as other than any finite part of the universe. Nevertheless, some parts of the universe can function as analogous to the being of the God who is pure Spirit. They enable us to make true statements about God, such as "God intentionally causes the universe to exist." This God is not *wholly* other, but is a mind-like supreme cause of an autonomous but dependent cosmos.

3

Analogies and Oxymorons

ANALOGY

It seems essential to say that we must speak of God analogically, for God, as the source of all beings other than God, as knowing all that can possibly be known, and as the most powerful being there could possibly be, must be radically different from finite beings. Yet I do not think it is true or plausible to say that all statements about God must be analogical, or that if one speaks analogically one must be saying something quite different from anything we might understand by the words we use. I think that some statements about God are fairly straightforwardly true, and that the meaning even of analogical words conveys something positive that we can understand, even though there is much that is not clear to us.

The Thomist account of analogy, as it was developed by Cajetan and others, apparently denies that this is the case. A good modern exposition of such an account is given by the Polish Jesuit Erich Przywara, who, in his *Analogia Entis*, first published in 1932 and translated into English in 2014 by John Betz and David Bentley Hart, defends a modern version of the Scholastic doctrine of analogy. As we shall see, when Dr. Pryzwara speaks of the relation of God and creation, he speaks of God as a fully existent and fully realized "essence," and creation as a set of partly realized essences. The "analogy of being," on his account, states that all created beings are "like" God in some way and to some degree (they "image" God), but God is infinitely beyond all beings, and to that extent infinitely unlike all created beings. This comports with the definition of the Fourth Lateran Council, that "between the Creator and the creature no similarity can be noted, however great, without compelling one to observe the greater dissimilarity between them."[1]

This apparently simple formula is loaded with hidden complexities, which Przywara exploits at great and extremely difficult length. Its basic affirmation is that created things do give some idea of what God is (God is not "wholly other"), but that nevertheless God is actually totally unlike ("beyond") all created things. The trouble is that this looks like a contradiction. If you say that "God is good," that seems to give some knowledge of what God is. But if you add that the word "good" is used in quite a different sense than any with which you are acquainted, you undermine that knowledge. I think you should really be saying that God is something like, but not totally like, what we understand by "good." But Przywara's account stresses the dissimilarity to such an extent that it fails to provide any positive information.

As it came to be understood in Scholastic theology, there are two main forms of analogical speech, usually called the analogy of attribution and the analogy of proportionality. The analogy of attribution has been explained by Aquinas by adverting to the word "health" as applied to humans, urine, and medicine. Humans are healthy; medicine can be called healthy as the cause of human health, and urine can be called healthy as a sign of human health. The word "health" does not mean the same in these three cases. Medicine is not "like" human beings in any way. If one used this to speak of God and creation, one might say "God is good" to mean that God is the cause of good things. But it would not follow that God is like good things in any way, and it would be clearer just to say that good things must have a cause, and that is God.

The obvious rejoinder is that there are lots of bad and neutral things in existence, too, so since God is the cause of all, it would be just as true to say "God is bad" or "God is smelly" (since God is the cause of smelly things). Unless one accepts Thomas' doctrines that causes must be like but greater than their effects, and that bad things are privations, and so not really caused by God, this use of analogy will be totally unconvincing.

---

1. Denziger-Schonmetzer, *Enchiridion Symbolorum*, 806, quoted in John Paul II, *Fides et Ratio*, para. 84.

An example sometimes used of the analogy of attribution is that of calling bread "good" by analogy with calling the baker "good." Here, the word good is being used in two senses. Bread is good if it tastes good, and is good for health. Bakers are good if they bake good bread. Bakers are not like but greater than bread in any important ways, so that does not seem helpful. In both cases "good" means something like "preferable" or "sets a standard of excellence." But the standards of excellence are quite different in each case. We don't care if bakers taste good and make us feel fit. We don't expect bread to take cookery courses. So it is not that the word "good" has different senses. It is rather that a general term of commendation is being used of different kinds of thing. As Peter Geach has argued, "good" is an attributive adjective. It does not change its meaning, but we evaluate things according to different standards, depending on what kind of thing we are evaluating.

If we apply this analysis to "God is good," we do not find that "good" is used analogously (in different senses). We find that we use different standards of assessment for God and finite creatures. We need then to ask what standards we have in mind. Is God worthy of reverence, of worship, of total life-commitment? Does God care for the well-being of creatures? Is God of supreme intrinsic value, worth-existing just because of what God is? Is God just and loving? There are a number of slightly different standards that might be used. If we reject all of them, the word "good" has lost its meaning; there is nothing we find commendable about God. If we accept one of them (say, Anselm's idea that God is the most intrinsically valuable being imaginable), then we have no need to apply to analogy. It makes no sense to say, "God is the greatest valuable being, but I do not mean by this anything that I think of as valuable." If what we say is to have any content, we must say that God is at least genuinely like what we think of as supremely valuable.

We do not have to say that this is exactly and exhaustively what God is, that we know the essence of God, that God has to conform to some humanly formulatable concept. That is what makes many theologians uncomfortable (especially Karl Barth). We can say, as Anselm actually did say, that God is much more valuable than anything we can imagine. But the point is that God is "more" valuable than we can imagine, not less, nor totally different. So it is just true that we think of God as at least as valuable (as "great") as the best we can imagine. No doubt God is much greater than we can imagine; but what we cannot imagine we cannot say either.

What theologians like Barth have apparently not perceived is that unless we believe God is worthy of worship and of our total loyalty, there is no reason to believe that anything God reveals to us is worth taking seriously. It is not good enough that we have some experience of a being who says, "I am totally worthy of worship, so listen to me," or we read some book (the Bible or the Qur'an or the Book of Mormon or the Guru Granth) that says or implies, "Everything in this book is to be obeyed." Why should we believe it? Only because we believe the one who speaks or writes is really worth listening to, and not because they say they are. Therefore, a belief that God, if there is a God, is supremely worthy of worship, and the belief that God really has said certain things, so they are worth believing, is presupposed to any rational acceptance of revelation.

It is not good enough to say that God is good, in a sense I cannot possibly understand, though God is really good. It is not good enough to say that God is good because we have some experience, or read some book, that says God is really good (in a sense I cannot understand). We need to believe that God is really worthy of worship, and cares for our well-being, before we can go on to add that God is, in the totality of the divine being, beyond all our categories of thought. The fact is, therefore, that however far beyond thought God is, that same God must also be in part within the reach of human thought, that we are right in thinking God is good, intelligent, just, and loving, a being who created the cosmos and is of supreme intrinsic value, and that we understand what these words mean.

What we do not understand and what we cannot imagine is what it is like to be such a being. What is it like to know everything knowable? To be able to create a cosmos? We have no idea what it is like. Nevertheless, we know what we mean when we say God knows, or God creates. God's knowledge is not like human knowledge, and God's creation is not like some humans creating a picture or piece of music. Yet we know that creating is intentionally causing something to be. So why call this analogical? If all it means is that God's causing a cosmos to exist is very different from Mozart causing a symphony to exist, we are well aware of that. It is a form of causing we will probably never fully understand, but we do understand what "causing" is.

The so-called "analogy of proportionately," the other main form of analogy in Scholastic philosophy, is no better. It says that: as goodness stands to human nature, so goodness stands to divine nature. But if we do not know what the divine nature is, we have no idea what such a relation

proportion-ality

would be. Whereas what we want is to say is that in some respects God is like humans—particularly, in respect of having knowledge, feelings, thoughts, and purposes. These things will be very different in God than they are in created persons, and they will be unique (not shared in that way by any other being). But in some form they will really be in God.

The problem with the "analogia entis" is that, at least in Przywara, it leads to a highly dubious idea of God. Because God contrasts with the separation of essence and identity in humans, it is asserted that in God essence and existence are identical. That is interpreted to mean that in God essence simply is existence. If this is taken in a strong sense—as it often is—this means that God just is existence or "Being," and is as such immutable and purely actual, without potentiality (which entails some essence that does not yet exist). All that God could be, God actually is.

I regard this as a major defect, as I believe that a being who could not ever be other than it is, who could not therefore ever do anything new, would not be the most supremely valuable being I can imagine, and so would not be worthy of worship. We are not supposed to know anything about the God "beyond human being," yet here we are told that God is immutable and impassible. How are we supposed to know that? I would quite understand being told that a supreme being would not change against its will, or for the worse, and that it would not be capable of being injured or destroyed by anything. But how could anyone know, of an ineffable being, that it could never will to do anything creatively new or to be passionately involved with a created world? These attributes, total immutability and impassibility, are purely philosophical speculations, which presume that such attributes are "greater"—more valuable—than their contradictories. I am not opposed to philosophical speculations, obviously. But I think these ones are incorrect. More to the point, they contradict the assertion that God is unknowable.

I do not believe God to be totally ineffable, so whatever I say about God may be inadequate, but it is meant to be true. I just have to do the best I can, and try to imagine the most perfect being I can. For me, that would be a being that is ever-creative and an abyss of potentiality for goodness and beauty.

The *analogia entis*, as propounded by Przywara, asserts that God is wise, but not in a sense I understand. What I would prefer to say is that God is wise, and I understand that perfectly. But what it is like for God to be wise I have little or no idea. God in Godself, the *ousia* of God, remains beyond

to great to be described in words

all human categories of thought. But God as God appears to us is truly wise, good, and loving, and we know what this means. It means that the cosmos is intelligible, formed to realize a good purpose, and that God cares for the well-being of creatures. Of course it does not tell us what exactly the intelligibility of the cosmos, the purpose to which it tends, and the way in which the well-being of creatures will be realized, consists in—it is for science and for revelation to aim at some understanding of those things.

These differences may seem not to be of great importance. Fr. Przywara and I both believe in the ultimate incomprehensibility of God, in love as the central characteristic of God's being as we know it, and in the truth of some statements about God. The differences emerge when it is said that God is pure actuality, pure essence, or is-ness. For that, I believe, really is in conflict with the Christian beliefs that God is self-giving love who becomes incarnate and wills to unite the cosmos to the divine life, a God who has a history and who realizes the supreme divine nature precisely in creative and redemptive activity, in Christ.

ESSENCE AND EXISTENCE

Erich Przywara argues that the phrase "in-and-beyond" holds the key to understanding human language about God. He analyses at length the distinction between essence (the form or essential nature of a thing) and existence (the fact of a thing's existence). Human beings, and all finite beings, are such that their essence is never fully existent or exemplified. The essential nature of humanity, for instance, lies ahead of all individual humans, as an ideal to be realized. None of us, except Jesus Christ, manifests humanity in its fullness. Also, our existence is not possessed by us or controlled by us. However, this tension between essence and existence, he holds, points towards a reality for which essence and existence are identical and self-sustaining. Whereas with finite things essence and existence are contingently related and non-identical, there is a reality for which essence and existence are identical. This is, of course, God. So we can speak of essence as "in-and-beyond" existence, in one case imperfectly and contingently manifested, and in the other case perfectly, necessarily, and indivisibly one.

There is a major logical problem with saying, of any being, that its essence and existence are identical. For most things, to state their nature (for instance, that humans are rational animals) is not to say whether or not they exist. Existence is the instantiation of a nature in some actual world.

It may be true of a particular human that it is instantiated in some actual world, but it is not part of the nature of humanity that is has to be instantiated in some world. (It is arguably part of the nature of humanity that it is capable of being instantiated in some world, and part of the nature of any individual human that it is not instantiated in every possible world.) Can it be part of the nature of some being, X, that it is instantiated in every possible world? It seems to me that it can. But one would still have to ask: what is the nature of that which is universally instantiated? It seems vacuous to say that its nature is just that it is universally instantiated. That is tantamount to saying that "that which is universally instantiated is universally instantiated," which conveys no information.

It follows that the essence and existence of X cannot be identical, in the sense that one term is equivalent to the other in every case. It can be the case that some essence is universally instantiated, but there must be more to the essence than universal instantiation, or existence in all possible worlds. In the case of God there is more, for God is supremely perfect and the intelligent cause of all but itself. Of course, Dr. Przywara would affirm this, too. But in that case I think it is misleading to say that God is simply "Being" (i.e., universal instantiation). Indeed, there is no such entity as "universal instantiation," even if some entity could logically be universally instantiated. Dr. Przywara is in my opinion smuggling into the notion of "Being" the very complex ideas of supreme perfection, wisdom, and causality. I have no objection to that, as long as it does not lead to saying such things as that the being in question is incapable of any sort of change.

"God is Being," for Przywara, means that God is all that God can be. There is nothing unfulfilled in the being of God. God is the "fullness of being." But again these superlatives disguise a nest of logical complexities. Can some beings be "fuller" than others, or are all beings real in their own distinctive way? Is there nothing at all that God could be, yet is not? Would this really be the most perfect imaginable state?

What is taking over at this point, philosophically speaking, is a Platonic reification of forms, especially of the transcendental forms of truth, beauty, and goodness. If one resists this Platonic move, one can still say that there are many sorts of beautiful thing, but they do not all participate in one supreme form (*eidos*) of beauty. Similarly, there are many sorts of particular beings, in rich variety, but they do not all participate in a supreme essence of Being, which actually exists in some ethereal intelligible world, beyond the world of particular things. And there are many sorts of goodness, of states worthwhile just for their own sakes, but they do not all participate in an essence of goodness.

If we reject the Platonic worldview, we may still speak of supreme beauty, but we will be speaking of a reality that is itself supremely beautiful, and is the source of all the hugely varied sorts of particular beauty, something that has an unlimited power (or potency) for emanating beautiful things and states. This source will be actual, not in the sense that it always is what it could ever be, but in the sense that it is endlessly capable of producing new forms of beauty. It is a reality that contains an infinite (limitless) potential.

The source of all beings will be able to produce endless forms of intelligible reality and endless forms of intrinsically worthwhile existents. It will be the source of all truth, beauty, and goodness. But it will not be an essence, a form, something in the end impersonal and immutable. It will be a personal reality, with thoughts, feelings, and intentions, filled with the power of originating new forms of being, of which we are one.

This calls for the replacement of the Platonic/Aristotelian world-picture by a more dynamic, fully personal conception of the nature of ultimate reality. It is not that the Platonic picture is wrong. But it reduces history and time, creativity and particularity, to the status of half-reality, and gives priority to the timeless, immobile, and unchanging. A more adequate view is also to be found in Plato, that time and change are fully real; they are "the moving image of eternity" (*Timaeus*), and their existence gives the eternal forms new creative sorts of embodiment. In Christian terminology, the incarnation of the Eternal in time is part of the essential nature of being. It is where new values are generated and developed, not a lamentable overflow of true reality into a world of shadows and illusions.

DAVID BENTLEY HART

David Hart is an Orthodox theologian who has little time for such "Hegelian" or late-Romantic ideas. He regards them as a theological "calamity," and holds that they do not just differ from the view he happens to hold, but that they embody deep and catastrophic misunderstandings of the Christian tradition, which threaten the collapse of the Christian faith completely.

In opposition to all such desperate theological tendencies (of which I am guilty), he writes that they all conclude with the absurd thought that

"God depends upon creation to be God and creation exists by necessity (because of some lack in God)."[2]

He thinks that people like me deprive God of true transcendence and completeness of being, in making God depend on a created world, and the necessity of creation undermines any sense of the gratuitous existence of the cosmos, which is a free and unpredictable manifestation of God's infinite love.

"The idea of a God who becomes through suffering passion . . . is simply a metaphysical myth."[3] That means, I think, that he does not agree with it. Like other writers I have discussed, he objects that mere monotheism sees God as a supreme being, whereas what he thinks of as a correct trinitarian view sees God as "the source of all being," not a being possessed of potential, "receiving his being from another . . . from being."[4] It should be obvious that any supreme being must itself *be*. But it is not at all obvious that it must receive its being from another, or that such a weird entity as "Being" is somehow prior to any existent being. "Being," like "running" or "singing," is not something that exists. A supreme being is precisely a being that does not receive its being from another. It exists by necessity, and is self-existent. But it is clearly existent. All Hart means is that God is not a dependent, created, being, and that is obvious.

Could such a supreme self-existent being be possessed of potential? Nothing known to me in Christian revelation answers this question. But as a purely philosophical opinion it seems to me that a being that is capable of new creative actions is more supreme than a being that cannot be other than it is. A truly creative being is in no sense "incomplete," for it possesses an unlimited power to do many good and creative things. It is infinite in the sense of being capable of endless creativity, as well as being unlimited by anything other than its own necessary nature.

A God who creates and becomes incarnate in creation is not improving or growing better. God is realizing God's creativity in an appropriate way. In a harmless sense God "becomes" as God acts in new ways, but God's eternal and necessary nature (which includes the capacity to become in these ways) does not change. God "depends on creation," but only in that if there were no creation, God would not be creatively active in the precise way that God is creatively active.

2. Hart, *The Beauty of the Infinite*, 157.

3. Hart, *The Hidden and the Manifest*, 45.

4. Hart, *The Hidden and the Manifest*, 46.

The sense in which God "depends" upon creation is ironically very like the sense in which Hart holds that the existence of God as Father "depends" upon the existence of God as Son and Spirit. For him, God would not be God unless the Son and Spirit existed as well as the Father. To put it brutally, there could be no Father without a Son. That entails that without a Son God would not be Father. But Hart apparently does not find that an unacceptable sense of dependence. The Father eternally and by necessity generates ("begets") the Son. The Father, in Hart's view, is what the Father is because the Son receives, returns, and shares the Father's love. But the Son is necessarily begotten, and does not beget himself.

In exactly the same way, if God's love is *agape* love, love of the other and the imperfect, then that love could not exist without a creation containing possibly imperfect creatures. But that creation in no way brings God into being, and it depends wholly upon God in order to exist.

I think that the intra-divine love that Hart supposes to exist is relatively limited, compared to the fully self-giving love that goes out to redeem an imperfect cosmos and unite it to the divine life. The intra-divine love is just of two "persons" who are as perfect (and necessarily so) as the Father. There is a two-fold limitation here. It is a love limited to just two "persons," which seems to me a very restricted sort of love. And it is a love limited to persons who cannot possibly reject the Father's love, who necessarily love the Father, and who are exactly like the Father, except for being "begotten" or "proceeding." It seems that this is also a very restricted sort of love, which is confined to loving beings exactly like oneself. It is also a strange sort of giving, receiving, and sharing love that involves no change (and therefore no responsiveness) of any sort.

How much greater is a love that extends to innumerable persons, many of whom are as different from the Father as they can manage to be, and gives itself to the uttermost to re-unite them with the one who loves them utterly? This is no dependence that arises from divine weakness or lack. On the contrary, it expresses limitless power constrained only by limitless love and wisdom.

The necessity of creation, therefore, does not arise from a lack in God, but from the fact that God's love by nature overflows to create persons drawn out of nothing who can come to share in God's love and joy. This love for creation is as necessary to the nature of a God whose love is not just limited to the divine being itself as is the love for other divine persons which, for Hart, is part of the necessary nature of God.

The Bible does not explicitly make any judgment on these matters. It does not say in what exactly God's almightiness and uniqueness consist; it does not say whether God necessarily or contingently creates a cosmos; it does not say whether or not God is affected by the free actions of creatures; it certainly never raises the question of whether God's nature is simple or not.

If the church, or some part of the church, has made decisions about these things, they should certainly be attended to carefully. My part of the church, at least, historically has held that councils of the church not only can err but have erred, even in things concerning God (Article 21 of the 39 Articles of the Church of England). I think that is right, but, unlike Hart, I am not accusing those who made such "errors" of simple misunderstanding or calamitous behavior. I just think that it is hardly surprising that the philosophical positions they adopted were of their day, and are subject to reformulation for good reason.

Early theologians loved oxymorons, the use of apparent contradictions to make points forcefully and memorably. They would speak of "the impassible becoming passible" and "the eternal being born." In this they were following the example of Jesus, who used hyperbole and oxymorons ("the first shall be last," and "you must hate your father and mother" being typical examples) in his teaching. But analytical thinkers have the job of teasing out the latent profundity behind the rhetorical contradictions. This is not difficult to do. Thus, one can construe the sentences above as: "The divine nature which cannot be changed by anything it does not will or permit can choose to add to itself a human nature capable of suffering," and "the Wisdom of God, which exists without beginning or end, can add to itself the transient life of a human being."

Can a changeless nature add to itself a changing and transient nature? There is no logical problem about this, if the changeless nature, consisting partly of dispositional properties like "love" and "wisdom" and "care for the welfare of others," is capable of realizing those properties in many diverse particular ways. One of those ways would be to take on some of the properties of persons in created time. Then the changeless property of "wisdom," for example, would be realized within the limitations of a created mind. This is a sort of *kenosis*, self-limitation, since it limits the operation of wisdom in a creaturely context. But it is equally an expression of divine power (a dispositional power that is never changed), for it realizes a new way of expressing the divine nature within a created and limited context.

Repeating early theological oxymorons is rhetorically and poetically effective. It would in my view be a mistake to try to take them literally, and provide an exposition of them which has to suppose that contradictions make sense.

I fear that Hart does that. The odd thing is that Hart's main motivation is the same as mine—to celebrate and defend the supremacy and changelessness of the divine love. That love is seen in human life as a totally self-giving entrance into the broken human world, in order that human lives should be enabled to participate in the divine love itself. On these things we both agree.

However, we have very different ways of spelling out the implications of these beliefs. For him, and for the early Christian tradition in general, the key model for divine love is love of changeless supreme beauty, untouched by any particle of sin or suffering or imperfection of any sort. His model of the Trinity is of the Father wholly giving his being in love to the Son, the Son wholly returning that love, and the Spirit filling out this beatific state with fellowship and joy.

In many patristic theologians, whom he cites, *agape* and *apatheia* are identified, and *apatheia* is said to be, not mere indifference, as the English word "apathy" might unfortunately suggest, but enjoyment and delight without passivity or passion. He describes it as "sheer yearning," or "divine ecstasy."[5]

There is an immediate problem with any such account when it is combined, as it usually was in patristic times, with an acceptance of divine simplicity, which would seem to rule out any "otherness" in God. But, Hart says, divine simplicity is capable of "including the fullness of relation and differentiation." This is the sort of oxymoron to which I object in any philosophical analysis, though I acknowledge its rhetorical effectiveness when left unanalyzed. On this model of intra-divine love, the Father gives "the entire gift of his being" and takes "pleasure in the other," in a fellowship of "regard, knowledge, and felicity."[6] I fail to see how this model avoids the charge of polytheism, of three divine beings in loving relation.

To me, there is here a confusion of two different sorts of love, the love of beauty, truth, and goodness, and the love of other persons, which is a delight in their presence, a cooperation in their actions, and a care for their well-being. The first of these is "beatific love." It is not between persons (in

5. Hart, *The Hidden and the Manifest*, 59.
6. Hart, *The Hidden and the Manifest*, 51.

the sense of different subjects of action and experience). It is more like love for an ideal or supreme case of something worthwhile. Plato's "Good" and Aristotle's "God" present that love very well, but they have little if any sense of God being a person in relationship to others, or of love as compassion and care.

Thus, one can say that God is threefold in *being* the Ideal, *knowing* the Ideal, and *loving* the Ideal. As Aristotle put is, God is *noesis noeseos*, the supremely beautiful thought that knows and loves that beauty for its own sake. There is little sense, however, in saying that the Ideal loves God in return, or that God gives his entire being to the Ideal. God just *is* the Ideal, as well as the knower and lover. I can see how this sort of beatific love could be called *apatheia*, because it is undisturbed by any possibly upsetting relationships to other persons, who have their own freedom and values, and it is pure and changeless.

If God is *agape* love, however, this is something different. It is love of what is truly *other* than God, not just love of the divine beauty itself. What is truly other is not God, thus that sort of love entails some form of created reality. The axiom that seems obvious to me, but not to Hart, is that *agape* love must be love of an other than the divine, other than even the most exalted self-love. That entails the necessity of some creation. Hart does not actually deny that. He says that God's love is essentially self-giving. As such, it naturally overflows into creation, not because it needs to, but because its fullness cannot be confined only to itself. We do not disagree about this. A created order does naturally and properly flow from God's self-giving love. Not only that, but in the incarnation "even the extreme of the *Kenosis*—crucifixion—is embraced within and overcome by the everlasting *kenosis* of the divine life."[7]

This is a conceptual move that I simply do not understand. Hart says that the infinite can "appropriate and accommodate the finite."[8] But he also says, "With or without creation . . . God would be fully God."[9] That entails, since God is changeless, that creation makes no difference to God. What can it mean, then, for God to appropriate, embrace, and accommodate the finite? Hart says that "the infinite divine image shows itself in one instance of the finite," but this is "not a change, but a manifestation."[10]

---

7. Hart, *The Hidden and the Manifest*, 56.

8. Hart, *The Hidden and the Manifest*, 53.

9. Hart, *The Hidden and the Manifest*, 51.

10. Hart, *The Hidden and the Manifest*, 53.

The problem is that, if there was no creation, God would not manifest or show Godself to anyone, and would not assume the finite into the divine, since there would be no finite reality. "Manifesting," "showing," "appropriating," and "assuming" are divine actions that would not occur without creation. But they are divine actions—created beings do not as if by accident or chance come to express the divine nature. God determines that they shall do so. This inevitably involves particular ways of expressing divine love. While that love may be changeless (God always indefectibly loves), the particular ways of expressing love must be different with creation than they would be without creation. They must be different if created persons are subject to sin and suffering than they would be if created persons had never sinned or suffered. The ways in which God's unchanging love shows itself must depend on whether there is a creation, and on what that creation is like. This is why what is often called "Rahner's Rule"—that the economic Trinity is the immanent Trinity and vice versa—is inaccurate. Whatever the Trinity is like without creation, it must differ from the Trinity that acts in particular ways within creation to judge and redeem it.

Hart is concerned that God should never participate in evil or make evil part of the divine being. So he objects to what he calls the "Hegelian" move of making evil a necessary moment in the temporal drama of God's redemptive love. I draw back from entering into a discussion of Hegel,[11] but I would say that if Christ takes suffering on himself, if he dies for our sin, that does not make Christ evil, or make evil necessary to God. What it does, however, is to affect God, to make it possible and actual that Christ suffers the consequences of evil, and overcomes them.

Hart himself must face the question of the origin of evil. Even if one ascribes all evil to malign moral choices, whether of humans or angels, one has to admit that the possibility of evil lies in God (there is nowhere else it could lie), and if evil comes to be, God sustains it in being. True, God does not will the evil, but if evil exists, it originates, as all created realities do, in God. Hart speaks as though God does not create evil, even as though evil does not really exist (it is a negation of good—though that does not mean it does not exist, for searing pain, which is surely evil, is a real and terrible aspect of human consciousness).

To say that evil arises from God by necessity (even if only conditional necessity, conditional upon the nature of the created order and the fact of human sin) is not to say that God is somehow evil. It is to say that God is

---

11. But see my chapter on Hegel, ch. 20, in *Religion and the Modern World*.

the source of all possibilities, good and evil, though God positively wills only good. God seeks, always and everywhere, to negate the power of evil and to turn it to good, and in this Christians trust that God will succeed.

There is a history of God's battle with evil, for God enters into a world of hatred and greed, to reform it and assume it to the divine life of love. The goal and end of this history is, as Hart says, *theosis*. As Gregory of Nyssa, quoted by Hart and one of my own favorite theologians, put it, the impassible was not changed when in Christ it assumed the changing, but the mutable "was changed into impassibility through its participation in the changeless."[12]

I think we need to construe this rather carefully. Firstly, God's changeless love is not altered with incarnation, but with the addition of a finite human life to the divine life there is a remarkable change in the way God's love is expressed. It is expressed in a human life that ends in apparent failure and pain. Secondly, we mutable beings are not "changed into impassibility," as though we ceased having a temporal existence, ceased learning and cooperating and sharing new experiences (Gregory is clear about this when he speaks of life after death in his *On the Soul and Resurrection*).[13] Rather, we are touched by God's changeless love, and that enables us to express that love in unique ways in our ever-changing lives. Gregory of Nyssa writes movingly of the way in which after physical death human souls continue an infinite, endless, exploration into God, moving from glory to glory as they grow in God.

We can, as Hart says, see salvation as "a matter of exchange."[14] God assumes our nature so that we can assume the divine nature. This does not mean that God changes into a human, or that we change into God. Nor does it mean that God changes in no respect, or that we cease being temporal beings. God establishes a union of divine life with the finite human reality of Jesus, so that this union can begin to grow in other human lives, as they allow the Spirit of Christ to work in them. Not only does Christ then live in us. As the New Testament puts it, we live in Christ, as all those who turn to Christ begin to form "the body of Christ," cooperating in realizing the purposes of God, as God's expressions and instruments in this small part of creation.

---

12. Hart, *The Hidden and the Manifest*, 54.

13. Translated by A. H. Williams in *The Nicene and Post-Nicene Fathers*, vol. 5.

14. Hart, *The Hidden and the Manifest*, 55.

It should be said, also, that the incarnation is not the only instance of God's loving and salvific action. It is the paradigm, in one human life, of God's universal cosmic action of uniting finite and infinite, so that finite things fully become expressions and mediations of divine infinity, and God's being is realized as *agapistic* love in that universal community of love, which is the end and goal of creation.

4

Being and Spirit

NECESSARY EXISTENCE

Thomas Weinandy is rightly concerned that God's essential nature is ontologically changeless and unalterable by creation. He puts the question, whether God is ontologically changeless or only ethically changeless, and insists that God can be ethically constant (in loving-kindness and faithfullness, say) only if he is ontologically changeless.[1] That is, it can only be guaranteed that God will always continue to love creatures if there is some ontological necessity and changelessness in God's nature. I believe he is right in saying that. It is not enough to say that God contingently is what God is, that God might have been otherwise, or might even not have existed. God exists by necessity with the nature that God has, and nothing can change or modify it.

The idea of "necessary existence" is a highly controversial one among philosophers. Some hold that it has no sense, but others, like Norman Malcolm, think that it is an idea that adds something to our definition of an object.[2] It is, in Alvin Plantinga's formulation, the idea of something that exists in all possible worlds. That tells us something interesting about an object—that there is no possible world in which it could fail to exist. In that sense it is, despite what Kant said, a determining predicate, one that

---

1. Weinandy, *Does God Suffer?* 63.
2. See Malcolm, "Anselm's Ontological Argument."

adds something to our knowledge of the object, and that is not analytically contained in the very concept of "God" (many theists, after all, deny it). I think it makes sense to say that God is such an object, that it is a good property for God to have, and that in some sense it is part of the essential nature of God that God exists by necessity with the nature God has. But does this entail that God's essential nature is, as Aquinas holds, *ipsum esse*, simple "existence-itself"? I doubt that this is plausible.

When we say that something exists, we use the word "exist" in various senses. We may say "Plato existed," and mean that there was such a person in a particular time and place. We may say, "numbers exist" (some, but not all, mathematicians do), and mean that whatever we think, numbers have real relations to each other, though they are neither in time nor in space. Some think that moral truths exist, meaning, roughly, that some moral statements are true, whether or not anyone accepts them. Some think that thoughts exist, and that they are not locatable in space, though they seem to take place in time. We may say that Pooh Bear exists, meaning exists in a book, or in someone's imagination.

There is not just one thing that "exists" means. To say "existence exists" is to speak, falsely, as though there was some one quality or property called "existence." Maybe there is a realm of mathematical ideas, another of ethical ideas, a realm of physical things, and a realm of thoughts, and they all have a set of members, defined in different ways (as numbers, physical objects, dream-contents, and so on). Then to say, "X exists"—or, what is the same thing, "X has being"—would be to say that X is a member of some definable realm (it need not be physical).

Logicians since Frege and Russell have pointed out that, even if "exists" is a grammatical predicate it is rather an unusual one. We can say that "A is red," and "red" is obviously a predicate, denoting a property of a thing, A. When we say, "A exists," "exists" is certainly a grammatical predicate. Logically, however, it is equivalent to the expression "for some x, x is A," or, in ordinary English, "There is an A." The predicate disappears, and is replaced by "There is," or by "for some x," or "there is an x, such that x is A." An important implication is that such expressions must be followed by a description of some sort. There must be something of a specific sort, which is said to "be."[3]

---

3. See the classic symposium on "Is Existence a Predicate?" by W. Kneale and G. E. Moore.

There are a number of sorts of thing X could be. If you say, "X exists," and if you want that statement to have a definite and clear meaning, you are committed to the view that X is a certain sort of thing. From this it follows that it does not make sense to say that "existence" or "being" can exist without being a certain sort of thing. For having "being" will mean "being a member of a set of sorts of thing." You would have to say what that set is, and what sorts of things are in it. "Being a member of a set" is an abstract concept for categorizing sorts of things. It seems, then, that "existence" or "being" is an abstract logical concept for classifying sorts of things. It is not part of the concept of anything whose existence is contingent. Kant was right about that, though he did not notice that "existence in every possible world" might be part of the concept of something.

Aquinas thinks of God as a pure self-existent form, a purely philosophical notion with Platonic-Aristotelian assumptions that are highly controversial. Aquinas says, "a form subsists as a thing . . . and is thus individual of itself."[4] This will not appeal to those who are suspicious of the idea that essences exist as individuals. He then says that "God is to be identified with his own essence."[5] God is a subsistent form, as are any forms that exist without matter (for Aquinas, like angels). But God's essence, or nature, unlike that of angels or other forms, is simply his existence.[6] "It is God's very nature to exist." Now, however, Aquinas takes a large logical leap, by concluding that God's *entire* nature is to exist, that "further specification is excluded by definition."

This is a huge leap, because God may have many properties (like wisdom, power, and love), and one of those properties, if it is a property, may be to exist by necessity. However, Aquinas holds that because God is simple, there is not a plurality of properties in God. Therefore, God has only one nature, which is simply *ipsum esse*, existence itself. But Aquinas also holds that the simple nature of God must in some higher and fully integrated manner contain all perfections. It would in this case be misleading to say that "being" was the only nature of God. It should rather be one of the things we have to talk about as distinct properties, though in God they are indivisibly united. However, Aquinas' commitment to divine simplicity leads him to say that God simply is the form of pure existence, actuality, or being.

4. Aquinas, *Summa Theologiae*, 3, 2.
5. Aquinas, *Summa Theologiae*, 3, 3.
6. Aquinas, *Summa Theologiae*, 3, 4.

To say that God is the essence of "existing" is to compound the logical problems concerning existence, if existence must be the existence of something. Aquinas' claim that in the case of God existence is itself an essence, gives the essence no definable content, so it is not at all clear what is being asserted. This is the core of Immanuel Kant's complaint that "existence" is not a "determining predicate," it is not part of the definable content of what one is asserting to exist[7]—though that is only true of contingent beings. To those influenced by Kant the Thomist idea of God must seem philosophically vacuous.

ACT AND POTENCY

The Thomist idea follows from the thesis that God is "simple," in the sense of containing no complexity at all. Thus, God is one simple pure and un-originated form or essence, and this essence is *ipsum esse*, being-itself. The argument goes like this: first he says that God, the ultimate cause of all, must be purely actual, for "actual existence takes precedence of potential existence."[8] This is an appeal to a basic intuition that possibilities need to be held in existence by something that is actual. They do not exist as something that is actual, but if they can be said to exist at all, they must exist in something that is actual. This is not something that is divinely revealed, and as an intuition it can be rejected without self-contradiction. But to many people it is intuitively appealing.

Then Aquinas moves straight on to the assertion that God is the first existent, so "in God there can be no potentiality." That does not follow. On the contrary, if all possibilities must be founded on something actual, the only inference one can draw is that there must exist one or more actual things on which all possibilities are founded. Supposing that there is just one first actual existent, that existent must, it would seem, contain all possibilities in itself. Far from God having no potentialities, God must contain *all* potentialities in the divine being.

The traditional "perfections" of God—wisdom, beauty, justice, mercy, love, power, and goodness—are interlinked in many ways, but there is little *a priori* reason to think that they are not different from one another in God, unless one thinks that for some reason God cannot be complex in any sense. The Christian God is said to be a Trinity, so it seems that

7. Kant, *Critique of Pure Reason*, Book 2, chapter 3, section 4, p. 282.

8. Aquinas, *Summa Theologia*, 1a, 3, 1.

a priori
deduced

the Christian God is essentially complex in some important sense. It is a complexity held within an integrated unity, and it does seem a rather foundational Christian ideal that a communion of being is something of great value, not an imperfection.

The doctrine that there is no complexity in God, and therefore no potentiality (for potentiality entails the possibility of change, which entails a possible succession of states in God, which entails that God is complex at least in some ways), is therefore based on intellectual intuitions that are disputable and implausible. Even if actuality is prior to potentiality, it does not follow that "in God there can be no potentiality." All that follows is that possibilities must be founded on something (or things) actual. A good example is the way in which possible futures can be contained as ideas in human minds. To exist as possibilities they must be founded on something actual, and in this case that actual thing is a human mind.

This example makes the point that while possibilities must exist in something actual, that thing need not be actual in *every* respect. In fact, the model of a mind conceiving ideas that it has the power to actualize, is arguably a more adequate model of God than the model of a pure form that contains every possible property "in a higher mode," all merged into one, in a reality that is incapable of any change at all.

DIVINE FREEDOM

It would indeed be a limitation on God to say that God is purely potential. But it would equally be a limitation to say that God is purely actual, if that means that all possibilities are ruled out for God, that there is nothing God can do other than what God actually does. I conclude that it makes sense to say that God exists necessarily, and that many divine properties are necessarily what they are. In particular, all possible states exist in God, and they are necessarily what they are. Their existence and nature are not matters of free divine choice. But are all divine properties necessary?

Aquinas says, "Why God does something is because he wills to do it; why he is able to do it is because such he is by nature, not because he wills it."[9] God has abilities to act that God does not will, but are just given in the divine nature. But God's particular willing could have been otherwise.

Yet Aquinas has held that God is supposed to be without potentiality, from which it follows that there is nothing God is able to do that God does

9. Aquinas, *Summa Theologiae*, 1a, 25, 5.

85

not do—there are no unactualized abilities in God. When it is said that God could have done otherwise, one can only mean (on Aquinas' view) that it is not logically contradictory to describe states of affairs that do not exist. But it is also not possible in fact for God to have brought about those states, since God is necessarily what God is, and the divine nature is simple, without change or complexity of any sort.

One can avoid this nest of difficulties by making God include temporality, by having an eternal and necessary divine nature together with a divine temporal agency that is conscious of and chooses between alternatives (potentialities) that are in the divine nature. If God can truly be said to be free, God must be a dynamic actuality, from whose being many forms can become actual. The fullness of God's actuality is such that from it new forms of being can flow—as Aquinas says elsewhere, supreme goodness by its nature overflows into many forms of actuality. God is actual and actualizing; unlimited potentiality is a necessary part of supreme actuality.

GOD AS BEING: JOHN MACQUARRIE

Aquinas' concept of God as "Being" has found influential modern supporters, though they often do not support all that goes along with his concept. Among the best known are Paul Tillich and John Macquarrie, who are both chiefly concerned to distinguish God from any "object" or finite entity.

In many ways I sympathize with this concern. But I fear that defining God as *ipsum esse* can readily lead to the idea of a morally indifferent and non-rational source of being. In the work of the philosopher Heidegger one can see that "Being" is the source of all beings, but it is not morally concerned or wise or purposive. It is perhaps this fact that led to Heidegger's inability to fully perceive the evil of Nazi ideology. Heidegger terms any attempt to turn Being into an object, much less a personal object, "onto-theology." He is right to object that theists have to add more than Being to their idea of ultimate reality, but wrong to think this is a mistake. In my view, it is a much greater mistake to think that the present participle "Being" can be, in defiance of the rules of grammar, used as an abstract noun, and taken to refer to some mysterious power or force that causes beings to exist. Heidegger's neologism "Being" is a much more mysterious and counter-intuitive notion than is the idea of an actual existent, God, which is the intentional and self-existent cause of all other beings.

To get an adequate Christian concept of God, one must somehow include purpose, wisdom, and value in the fundamental concept, and it is hard to see how calling God "Being-itself" does so. Purpose, wisdom, and value are qualities of mental agents, and however much greater than mind God is, such mental (spiritual) qualities must at least be correctly ascribable to God. The Christian God must be thought of as a God of love, and if that is the case it is not enough to say simply that God is "Being-itself." Love is a personal property, and "Being" does not seem to be personal at all.

Macquarrie at least defines what he means by "Being." He says Being is not an object, "a thing that is."[10] It is "the act or state or condition of being," a sort of energy that makes things be. My initial reaction to this is to say that it is an unnecessary addition to any respectable ontology, or list of things that are. Actually, it could not be in such a list, since if it were, on Macquarrie's hypothesis it too would require a preceding "energy" that made it be. If things exist, then they are. They do not require an additional mysterious force that makes them be.

In any case, if there is anything that makes things be, then whatever it is must have the power of bringing-to-be, of originating objects. It must have ultimate causal power. Whatever has the power to make things actual must itself be actual, and that actuality must be underived. Logically, it follows that there is something actual that has the power to make other things actual. So, despite what Macquarrie says, what he calls "Being" *is* "a thing that is." If one made a list of the sorts of entities that exist, one would have to include some actual existent entity that is not derived from anything else, and that has the power to bring other beings into existence. It possesses being in a way that no created object does, as an essential and underived property, but it still possesses being. It is a pointless move to say of everything that something must "let it be," for that something must itself be, if it is to be able to let anything else be.

Macquarrie's account of being differs from that of Aquinas, because he thinks that "becoming must be included in being as well as distinct from it."[11] Aquinas thought of God as *actus purus*, the pure and unrestricted act of being. But he also thought that this excluded all becoming, all potentiality. Macquarrie objects that we must not think of being as "static, changeless, and undifferentiated." He also thinks that "Being gives itself in and through

10. Macquarrie, *Principles of Christian Theology*, 98.
11. Macquarrie, *Principles of Christian Theology*, 101.

its appearances, and nowhere else."[12] So there have to be appearances of being. Being does not just exist in splendid isolation, complete in itself. It lets beings be, and appears in different degrees of plenitude. Being becomes present and manifest in different degrees in and through the beings, in different degrees, of which the greatest is personal being.

Macquarrie speaks not just of "Being," but of "Holy Being." An appropriate religious attitude to Holy Being is one of "acceptance and commitment," of faith and hope. One should learn to accept finitude, transience, and mortality,[13] and one's own place in the world. And one should commit to an authentic possibility of personal fulfillment, in the belief that such fulfillment is possible. If this is so, Being generates beings of a certain sort, makes it possible for them to come to fulfillment, and demands that they do so. Thus, Being contains moral demands or ideals, and has purposes for the world of beings. Ideals exist, and objects exist to realize them in freedom.

This is not just an act that brings objects of all sorts into being. It requires a being that is conscious, a being that demands, a being that holds out a promise of fulfillment, and a being that can transform one's existence from despair and anxiety to hope and acceptance. In speaking of Holy Being one is saying that a specific attitude of acceptance and commitment is appropriate to Being. This is more than "letting-be"; it is also defining authentic possibilities and shaping events to enable them to be realized. God is a source of moral ideals and a purposive moral power that shapes the future to accord with those ideals. This may not be much like a human person, for human persons do not embody moral ideals or have ultimate control over their future. But it is also not much like a featureless "source of beings." It has a character, a definite nature, consisting of ideals and a form of purposive causality. It seems correct to call this *a sort of object*, though one that is non-physical, necessary, and uncreated. It has what we can recognize as mental powers (formulating ideals, having a purpose, and shaping the future are mental powers), though far beyond those of any created being.

Rowan Williams makes a rather similar point when he remarks that a mere additional and "rival fact" could not make an unconditional claim upon us.[14] It is, however, a rather odd thought that "mere facts" cannot evoke in us certain appropriate types of affective response. Of course, we

---

12. Macquarrie, *Principles of Christian Theology*, 102.

13. Macquarrie, *Principles of Christian Theology*, 69.

14. Williams, *Christ the Heart of Creation*, 271.

can make lists of "mere facts" in which we do not have much personal interest, but that is a very sophisticated activity. When we apprehend objects in the world, our apprehension usually carries with it distinctive attitudinal and behavioral responses. When we apprehend a crouching tiger, we apprehend something fearful, something that affects us immediately. Our apprehension is not just neutral, as if waiting for some later purely subjective emotional response from us. So, if we apprehend another person we may immediately find them fearsome or attractive, and seeing persons in pain does make a claim for our active response. We may ignore that claim, but it is part of our initial apprehension, and not an optional addition to it.

If, in claiming to apprehend God, we experience a personal presence of supreme wisdom and love, it may and ought to claim our unconditional loyalty. In fact, one important reason for grounding moral obligations in the personal being of God is that the love we naturally feel when truly confronted with a personal God of supreme wisdom, beauty, and power is the strongest reason for obeying the moral law that God enjoins. We obey the law, not out of fear, but because we love the law-giver. Belief in the fact that God exists and loves does make an unconditional claim upon us, whereas I am not at all sure that belief in such a vague and speculative "Being that lets all things be" would make any sort of claim upon us at all.

EXISTENTIAL VALUES

Revealingly, Macquarrie does not like an "I-Thou" model for the relationship between God and creatures. He points out that God is not physical, as humans are, that there can be no real mutual reciprocity between creator and creature, and "in revelation we do not know another being, but simply being."[15] This devaluation of personal relationship does not seem adequate to much Christian experience, which does find itself in relation to God as Father, which is certainly a personal relationship. God is not a human person, has no body, and is dimensionally more powerful, wise, and good than any human person. But it does not seem to be true to Christian experience to say that God has no personal properties. Indeed, according to Christians, God can take a finite form, and as I have just argued, God is "another" being, though obviously not a physical or created one, limited to our spacetime.

15. Macquarrie, *Principles of Christian Theology*, 84.

God can, if the biblical record is correct, create physical appearances that communicate something true of divinity. Persons are a particularly rich and appropriate vehicle of communication, both human and divine. So I think an "I–Thou" model is appropriate, even though with the necessary qualification that what humans encounter as "Thou" vastly exceeds the limits of its appearances. Still, the appearances may be genuine, and what goes beyond their limits is the un-nameable transcendent. It does not help define the un-nameable to call it "Being," "the One" or "the Real." There is that which is beyond, but for followers of the Abrahamic religions many of the appearances of God to the patriarchs and prophets give rise to true descriptions of what it truly is in relation to us, even though if we took those appearances as totally adequate expressions of the being of God in itself we would be sadly mistaken.

Aquinas holds that "eternal life . . . consists in seeing the divine essence."[16] It must be possible, then, for humans to "see" the divine essence, though not by the senses or the power of natural reason, and not during this earthly life (except by some miraculous act of God). What is required is that God will shape our understanding to be like God in some fashion, and though we will never comprehend God fully, we will have an immediate and intellectual apprehension of the divine essence.

This means that God is not unknowable in principle. God can be apprehended, though probably beyond earthly life, as containing, as possibilities, the perfections of all possible things, as being itself of supreme value, and as the self-existent cause of all. If this is what Aquinas means by *ipsum esse*, I think virtually all theists would agree. My argument simply is that God has properties that God without creation would not possess, though they do not change the eternal nature of God as supreme value and cause of all. However, to say that God is "pure Being" does not seem to be the most adequate way of describing the nature of the divine. The concept of "being" is too abstract and devoid of substantial content to be adequate to characterize a reality the fullness and magnificence of which is such that it is greater than and the source of all created realities.

Macquarrie contrasts "traditional theism," which makes God "an exalted being beyond the world,"[17] with "existential-ontological theism," which holds that being itself is holy, present, and manifest, and gives hope for fulfilling the potentialities of selfhood. He insists that this is not

16. Aquinas, *Summa Theologiae*, 1a, 12, 4.

17. Macquarrie, *Principles of Christian Theology*, 106.

pantheism, which identifies God with an object (i.e., the whole universe as an all-inclusive object). God is transcendent, yet that transcendence is present and manifest in and through all beings, and only there. He says, "What is revealed is not another being, over and above those that can be perceived by anyone."[18] We see the same things in a different way, in depth. We see an extra dimension, present and manifest in various degrees. What we see is that there is value in being, that it presents a demand to live authentically, and that human existence, or that which conditions human existence, makes such authentic living a real possibility, that it has a goal. These are all remarks about the nature of reality, as it is or as it can be experienced by humans—this is the "existentialist" element in Macquarrie's thought.

But we cannot avoid two major questions: "Are there really objective values and ideals that can be felt as genuine demands on human life?" and "Is there some goal for human existence that can be attained?" Is there a moral teleology in nature, or is that an imaginative invention with no basis in objective reality? This is a question of fact, though not one that can be decisively answered by empirical investigation. The ontological question cannot be avoided: if there are objective ideals and purposes in reality, how are we to understand the nature of that reality? It seems to me that the most coherent possibility is that there is a unitary reality that contains moral ideals, that constitutes reality so that those ideals are achievable, and that has causal power to ensure they are achieved.

It is true that the human search for God is not a search for an additional object, which might be discovered, perhaps through some sort of intellectual argument. It is a search for the innermost character of human existence. It is concerned with the discernment of value and purpose in human life, and therefore in the cosmic context of which human life is part. But I do not think this insight is best protected by speaking of the ultimate reality just as "Being." One can, I think, speak more fully and informatively of a cosmic mind, which is indeed the underlying reality of all existence, though it has become largely obscured from us by human greed, hatred, and ignorance. What we are called to see is a mind of supreme wisdom and love, of demand and promise, which is the true reality veiled by our perceptions of a world of objects to be used and enemies to be confounded, a world seemingly ruled by a combination of mere chance and blind necessity.

One can have a sense that certain places, people, or events, seem to mediate a spiritual power, a sense of transcendence, of value and meaning,

18. Macquarrie, *Principles of Christian Theology*, 80.

that draw from us a renewed sort of commitment and purpose. It is as if a veil has for a moment been drawn aside to show a deeper reality, but one that is disclosed in and through the everyday objects of our experience.

Perhaps Aquinas' affirmation of God as a pure actuality where all things that seem to us to be distinct properties are united in a greater and indivisible whole, where all perfections are transcended at a maximal point beyond description, and where there is only one unlimited actuality, is not the terminus of a logically valid argument, but a gesture towards the "infinite ocean of being" of which Boethius writes. What can then happen, especially when handled by less subtle minds, is that the fullness from which all words turn back can be turned into a restrictive positive dogma, as if the reality that cannot be grasped by thought had at last been definitively described.

What is required is the negation of the negation of all describable properties. Then one might say that God, the ultimate being, is not potential in the sense that it lacks something of its perfection that has yet to come into being. It is not complex in the sense that it is an assemblage of distinct and separable parts. It is not changeable in the sense that there is something more perfect that it is yet to become. And it is not passible, in the sense that something could injure or destroy it. Yet all these assertions have also to be negated. For God is the creative source of the infinite forms of reality, not a being unable to do anything new. God is the archetype of infinite worlds, not a being unable to apprehend innumerable finite forms of beauty and understanding. God is acutely responsive to creation, not unable to appreciate its happiness and grieve over its sorrow. And God's love is passionate and particular, not a generalized but inactive pity that never moves to action.

When Macquarrie speak of "Being," he wants to stress that God is not some sort of finite object existing outside the universe and interfering in it occasionally, which can only be conjectured by abstract argument. He wants to speak of the inner character of this very world in which we exist, and claim that it has an inner depth, that it contains presence, demand, and goal, which can be apprehended by overcoming the egoistic self and becoming open to the attracting power of beauty, truth, and goodness. In religions, this attractive yet demanding power becomes known in key experiences where the veil of the sense-world is drawn aside, and its deeper nature is revealed.

This is, I suggest, the "infinite and eternal" of which Schleiermacher wrote, though he later, partly in response to accusations of pantheism, re-phrased such perceptions as a sense of "absolute dependence," to make it clearer that he was not just speaking of the universe in its totality (which his phrase, "the Whole" might have implied). It is more like the vision of changeless beauty that transfigured Augustine and is the heart of the mystical quest.

There are, nevertheless, significant differences in these varied gestures towards the unknowable. With Hegel and Macquarrie the values of free creativity, relationship, particularity, development, and history, are given greater prominence than in ancient Greek philosophical thought. The mystical quest is not seen as a "flight from the alone to the Alone," but as a search for the temporal embodiment of eternal values, the inbreaking of the eternal into the world of time.

Macquarrie sees Being as necessarily manifest in particular beings, whereas Aquinas sees Being as complete in itself without creation. However, is that difference as great as it seems? Both believe that "the Word became flesh." For Thomas, that caused no change in God, but God changed the human nature of Jesus in a radical way. For Macquarrie, God changes by becoming flesh, but such changes only disclose the eternal nature of the divine in temporal forms; they do not change that nature. The fact is that for Thomas, when God changed human nature, God in a sense did something that God would not have done had there been no creation. And for Macquarrie, God did not change the divine nature as wisdom and love when that nature was manifested in diverse ways in temporal forms.

I have been critical of the Thomist way of characterizing God, suggesting rather unkindly that it proceeds from implausible axioms to a virtually vacuous concept of Being. That is not because I am critical of traditional Christian faith, but because I am critical of Aristotelian philosophy, and so cannot see it as helpful in an attempt to construct a coherent idea of God for twenty-first-century thought. But theologians rightly wish to have such a coherent idea, and since the Bible does not provide it, they have to use some philosophical system as its basis. There is no modern philosopher who has the reputation that Aristotle had for medieval thinkers. So we just have to do the best we can, using whatever concepts seem to help us best in understanding Christian faith.

I agree completely with Thomists when they say that God is passionately loving and also changeless in perfection. What I disagree with is that their adoption of Platonic and Aristotelian ideas of perfection has forced them into an unduly paradoxical way of spelling out this twofold nature of God. I am unable to grasp how one can think both that the being of God is necessary and does not change at all, and also think that God passionately loves a contingent creation. I have argued that it is less paradoxical, yet not at all reductive of the divine mystery, to say that the changeless divine nature, because it is partly constituted by dispositional powers, is precisely manifested in creative acts of responsive relationship, of self-giving *agape* love. The divine becomes incarnate in time in order to include the temporal within the divine being itself, giving it a share in the divine nature (2 Pet 1:4), and thereby realizing what has always been potential in the divine nature, that the purpose and goal of creation is a communion of beings in conscious relationship, within the all-inclusive reality of God.

5

Finite and Infinite

ROWAN WILLIAMS

I have argued that logically speaking God is a sort of thing. God may be much more than a mind, as we know and imagine minds, but it is at least true that God thinks and intends, and these are mental properties. God is "mind and more," but God is at least mind. It is commonly said that God knows everything that can be known; God is more powerful than any other being could possibly be; and God is supremely happy or blissful. All these attributions entail that God thinks, acts, and feels. God in Godself has no physical form, but can create physical forms that suggest and often express God's wisdom and loving-kindness.

If these things are true of God, then God belongs to the genus of "uncreated minds who are creators of everything other than themselves," a genus that necessarily contains only one member. God is also, as well as being the creator of all, a cause among others within the physical universe. God's appearing to Moses in the burning bush is a physical phenomenon caused by God, which no physical causes could bring about by their own created powers. Even more importantly, the sinless person of Jesus who could still storms and walk on water could not have been generated by the normal powers of physical causation placed in nature by God. There is here a particular causal influence beyond all created natural powers.

One might naturally feel like saying that sinlessness and extraordinary mental powers are not contradictions of human nature, but completions of human nature as it was meant to be. These are forms of mental causality showing the power of mind over the physical world and over internal temptations to self-centeredness and pride. Jesus' mind was enriched and expanded to an extraordinary degree, by the causal power of the uncreated mind of all.

This seems to be the view taken by Rowan Williams, and it is a much more illuminating view than the idea that Jesus was just a supernatural intrusion into the natural world, who, as divine, has little in common with more normal human beings. Williams' account, however, is in my view compromised by his apparent acceptance of a generally Thomist view of God, seen through the lens of Austin Farrer. This leads him to say such things as that God cannot be seen as a member of a genus, as a cause within the universe, or as any sort of particular entity, thing, or object. I think these claims result from concentrating on ancient Greek philosophical assumptions, which Aquinas accepted, but which are, as I have tried to show, in tension with biblical ideas of God.

For example, Rowan Williams says that God and the created universe cannot be added together so as to make two things. But is this the case? Well, they are obviously not two things of the same sort. Yet there certainly are two *types* of things, and an atheist will be positing some new fact about the types of things that exist, if she comes to believe in God. In his beautifully written book *Christ the Heart of Creation*, Rowan Williams fears that such an admission will somehow limit the freedom and power of God. He particularly fears what he calls a "competitive" account of divine action. This seems to be the view that when God acts nature must cease to act, and when nature acts, God cannot act. Thus, God's actions could only interrupt nature, and replace natural causality by occasional divine acts. Dr. Williams rightly points out that this is an unhelpful view of divine actions. He writes, "God's transcendence of the categories of the finite" entails "the essentially non-competitive character of the juxtaposition of divine and created."[1] There is a stronger and a weaker interpretation that one can made of this assertion.

The weaker interpretation notes that God is not a finite entity within the universe, therefore God's actions are not subject to the causal laws of the natural world. The stronger interpretation, which I think Dr. Williams

---

1. Williams, *Christ at the Heart of Creation*, 64.

takes, is that God is not a thing of *any* sort—"God is not a case or instance of anything"[2]—whereas to me it seems obvious that God is a case, the only case, of being a creator of everything other than itself. Therefore, Dr. Williams says, God cannot be a cause of events in the natural world. "The believer does not claim that there are any more facts in the universe than the unbeliever allows, . . . their difference is not about the presence in the world of some extra agency called divine."[3] But some believers, anyway, think that miracles occur, that a man appeared after death, and even that a virgin conceived a son. These are all facts that most unbelievers will not allow. As the word "miracle" implies, these are facts that are not explicable in terms of any known laws of physics. They are brought about by God, and only God (or possibly some other spiritual agency) could bring them about. Does this mean that divinely caused events "compete" with naturally caused events?

Dr. Williams seems clearly to affirm that God does make some sort of causal difference. God "extends," "enlarges," "opens," "enhances," "transfigures," "organizes," "modifies," "shapes," and "fulfills" human lives. These are all words that Dr. Williams uses, in different places, with regard to divine action. All of them entail some sort of causal influence, some difference that God makes to the world in addition to whatever the laws of nature have the power to bring about. He wishes to stress that such influence does not interrupt nature, but works towards its completion. For nature is intended to be a sacrament of the divine, manifesting and mediating the divine wisdom and love. Thus, when God makes nature more able to do this, that is not "competing" with nature, but completing nature.

God enhances, and does not replace, human freedom. Negative freedom takes as its motto, "Leave me alone," and thus excludes God from having any influence on human nature. Positive freedom, however, is expanded by relationship with other personal beings. For example, I am only free to write and perform a symphony if I cooperate with an orchestra. I am not free to do it on my own. So human freedom to attain the goal of created human nature, which is to be united in love to God as well as to other created beings, cannot be achieved on one's own. It requires the cooperation of others and, most importantly, of God. As St. Augustine put it, God alone makes it possible for humans to achieve the goal that God demands.

It needs to be remembered, however, that not all God's recorded acts are of this positive nature. The world is estranged from God—"he came

---

2. Williams, *Christ at the Heart of Creation*, 113.

3. Williams, *Christ at the Heart of Creation*, 270.

to what was his own, and his own people did not accept him" (John 1:11). Humans are often evil and oppose God's will and purpose. It cannot be expected, then, that God will enhance or enlarge their powers for evil. God will seek to frustrate and diminish their powers, influencing, though not determining, them so that their acts will eventually end in failure and self-destruction. So it is that some divine influences do not complete nature, but do indeed compete with nature, insofar as nature is corrupted and alienated from God.

In such cases, too, one might well want to say that God does not simply interrupt nature. God will influence the way things go so that evil does not fully accomplish its goals, and so that in the end evil will be completely eliminated. Divine influence is always oriented towards goodness, but that means that often it will also be directed to frustrating evil. In both cases, it may be better to speak of "influence" rather than determining causality. God does not just step in and make people saints instantaneously, and God does not eliminate all evil just as it is about to occur. It looks as though efforts towards goodness are supplemented, and efforts towards badness are frustrated, so that the world may be liberated from its alienation from God.

Such divine action is as much a supernatural act as is the phenomenon of the burning bush. It surpasses normal human or natural powers, even though in the case of humans, doing so makes them more like what they were always meant to be—or in the negative case prevents them being totally lost to the divine love. Dr. Williams is concerned to say that in the case of Jesus, God does not just act from time to time, but that the whole life of Jesus is one divine act. Jesus' wisdom and compassion were always supplemented by a wisdom and love beyond normal human capacities, and his physical powers were supplemented in a way that enabled him to perform miraculous acts. Divine wisdom, power, and love were added to the human powers of Jesus, not sometimes but always throughout his life, to give them the efficacy they had, and make him unique among humans. These additions were always meant to be a proper part of human nature, and may be so in some future state, but the fact of "fallenness," of pride, hatred, and greed that have alienated humans from God have made them seem additional to the normal powers of estranged humanity. Jesus is restoring humanity to its divinely intended status, not just adding supernatural powers that from time to time interrupt the course of nature.

This means that God is doing something in Jesus that God would not have done without creation, and that God would not have needed to do if humanity had not become estranged from God. God is making it to be the case that a temporal life authentically expresses the divine nature in a finite human form. If this is something that God really does, then God really acts temporally, or causes this temporal sequence to exist as it does. Even if you think that God produces the whole universe by one non-temporal act, God will directly cause an increase in Jesus' powers that is not explicable just by reference to general laws of nature alone. God acts so that this beyond-natural-law event occurs at time T. Of course, God is acting all the time, in maintaining the universe. But some specific events are such that they do not occur solely by the operation of natural laws. It is reasonable to say that in such cases God acts in a distinctive, not scientifically explicable, way. Even if there is just one divine act of creating the whole of spacetime, within that spacetime there are sub-acts that can only be explained by reference to non-natural causality. In that sense, God acts within the universe in a distinctive way. The main difference from the burning bush case is that whereas God can just make the bush burn and not be consumed, God does not just make Jesus do what Jesus does. Rather, God by causal influence enables Jesus to do what Jesus himself decides to do, and what may have been a natural human power if humans had not fallen.

In the case of Jesus, of course, God also makes it the case that Jesus' life as a whole and in all its details is so "attuned" (Dr. Williams' word) to the divine will that Jesus becomes the temporal expression of the eternal Word of God, and thereby a revelation of the divine nature in a fully human body and soul.

This entails that God is a causal agent who acts in spacetime (God makes something, some specific thing within spacetime, to be the case that would not be the case without specific divine action). This is not to say that God is confined to or limited by spacetime. It is to say that the creator of spacetime can make specific events within spacetime revelations or disclosures of the divine will and purpose for creation. God truly acts in spacetime. This is an additional causal factor—the word influence seems to be appropriate—to the laws of the physical universe.

Since Dr. Williams writes so eloquently of this, I am puzzled why he should say that the life of Jesus is not "an episode in the life of a heavenly subject."[4] It is, after all, the Word of God who acts in Jesus. The attunement of Jesus' life to the divine will is not a mere coincidence, whereby the laws of nature *happen* to coincide with the divine will. God ensures that parts of

4. Williams, *Christ at the Heart of Creation*, 10.

nature express the divine will, and that some parts of nature (like the life of Jesus) do so more authentically than others (like the life of a mosquito). Moreover, it is part of the Christian hope that at some future time (even if it is a time beyond the historical time of this physical universe) all things will be united in Christ. That can only happen by specific divine actions, subordinating (or "opening") the laws of physics to the demands of morality and happiness (as they are plainly not subordinated at present). Such actions are episodes in the temporal involvement of the Word in creation. These episodes would not exist if there were not a creation, and if humanity had not fallen, and if humanity was never to be reconciled to God.

There is a puzzle about saying that God acts in time, however. It may seem to confine God to our time and make God subject either to improvement or decay—both impossible for a perfect being, it may seem.

Thomas Weinandy is concerned that God should not be subject to time, to emotional fits, to growth and decay. I agree that God is not subject to growth and decay in time, for God does not get more or less perfect as time goes on. God changelessly remains perfect in love, wisdom, and compassion. God is not subject to any irrational floods of emotion, as humans often are. If so, God does have affections or feelings, though they are always under divine control, perfectly rational, wise, and loving. I am in total agreement with Weinandy that "There is no fluctuation or change within God which could in any way alter his comprehensive goodness and consummate love."[5] Yet if God truly assumes a new mode of existence in the incarnation, this will make a difference both to the expression of divine perfection and to divine feeling.

If humans fall into sin, God's love will be concerned to correct the human will, whereas if humans turn to goodness, that same divine love will rejoice. It is not enough to say that the love remains the same, while all change is in the object loved. Concern for a person's welfare will lead to differing feelings and actions in regard to that person.

Dr. Weinandy himself quotes Tertullian, who wrote, "While God himself does not change, the mode of the expression of his goodness changes."[6] To put it in the slightly different terms I have used, God in Godself, especially in God's essential and eternal properties, does not change. It is the actual expressions of those properties in specific causal acts that change. As Dr. Weinandy says, in the incarnation, God "assumes a new mode of

5. Weinandy, *Does God Suffer?* 110.
6. Weinandy, *Does God Suffer?* 101.

existence."[7] Assuming a new mode of existence is a real change, an actualization in time of an eternal possibility in the divine mind.

It is not enough to say that God does not change at all in "becoming incarnate," while all changes are in the human nature of Jesus. If God causes those changes, as God does, then God acts in a new way, but that new way does not change God's love for humanity or for Jesus. We might even say that love that is not expressed is only embryonic and incomplete love. Love that does not respond to its changing object in changing ways is abstract and indifferent.

The fact that God changes in relation to the world does not mean that God is an object within the world. A Christian must say that, as creator, God cannot be classified as one object among other objects, objects that are created. As Aquinas put it, God does not belong to any created genus, a class of which there might be other members. Yet this remark, for a modern logician, is very misleading.

Consider the case of human beings. They belong to the genus of animal, to the genus of living organisms, to the genus of physical objects, and to the genus of existent entities. They belong to many genera, at various levels of generality. None of these, taken either separately or together, would give a sufficient definition of a human person, but they do give correct if partial descriptions of human persons. So God belongs to the genus of thinking purposive beings and to the genus of non-physical entities and to the genus of superhuman entities, though none of these give a sufficient definition of God. If one goes on to say that God knows everything and intentionally creates everything other than God, then God still belongs to a genus, but it is a genus that necessarily has only one member. God is the one and only uncreated mind. God is like some created things in being a mind, but unlike them in being a supreme and uncreated mind.

One reason why Aquinas holds that God cannot belong to a genus is because, he says, that would make the genus prior to the being of God. Also, God is identical with divine existence, and existence is not a genus anyway.[8] However, these arguments depend on a quasi-Platonic thesis that types (natures; eide) have independent reality, and even that they are in some way more real than the particulars that instantiate them (in The Republic Plato notoriously claims that the nature of "bedness" is more real

7. Weinandy, Does God Suffer? 104.
8. Aquinas, Summa Theologiae, 1a, 3,5.

than particular beds, which are only half real).[9] It is worth noting, however, that Plato himself undermines this claim in the *Parmenides*, so it can hardly be called definitively Platonic. Among theologians Anselm, nevertheless, uses a similar argument when he holds that ideas in God have more reality than particular existent things. As for the claim that "existence" is not a genus, that suggests that "existence" is not a type of thing or property at all. In other words, it is not a form or essence, and so should not be used to say what the essential nature of anything is. If that is so, it should not be logically possible to say that God is the pure and simple form of existence, especially if God is without any other distinguishing characteristics.

Presumably the ideas of all possible particular states, and of all possible sets, exist in God. But they are not entities external to God that limit God in some way. They are more like characteristics of the divine nature. As uncreated mind, God contains the idea of all possible states, and therefore of all possible natures. Probably the set of all possible states is necessarily what it is (since if something is ever possible, it is always, eternally, possible). While God does necessarily conceive of all possible natures, this is not an external limitation on God. It is an integral part of the necessary nature of God, as uncreated supreme mind. Thus classes, or genera, are not prior to God. They are conceptual forms contained in the mind of God. You might then not want to say that "God belongs to a genus," as though God belonged to some reality that is other and perhaps greater than God. But you should say that there is a true conceptual description of God, which is that God contains the conceptual forms of all possible things. That is, the concept of God defines God as a sort of thing, though that sort of thing (a being in some sense omniscient) is very different from finite created minds.

A CONTINGENT UNIVERSE?

It seems plausible to say that the world is contingent. Perhaps it did not have to exist at all; or perhaps some world had to exist, though there are real alternatives to this one. Within this world, humans did not have to sin; they could have obeyed God. But they did what God did not determine them or want them to do, and what God had commanded them not to do.

For this view, it would be odd to say that God commanded people to do something that God then caused them to disobey (for God implanted in them the desire to disobey). The logic of a command is that it tells people

9. Plato, *The Republic*, Book 10.

to do something that they can do, but do not have to do. People can weigh the command against their desires, and choose which to follow. On this "libertarian" view of freedom, nothing in the past determines what their choice will be. They envisage possible futures, and decide which to actualize. Being undetermined by the past does not mean that choices are arbitrary or random. There exist definite limiting factors, which means that only a finite number of alternatives are possible on any one occasion. The selection of an envisaged future goal because it is thought to be of value is not a random selection. Nor is it a selection determined by laws of nature. It is a selection made by understanding, imagination, personal evaluation, and creative decision. These are mental attributes, not properties of purely physical objects.

On this picture, God, knowing all possible futures, and correctly evaluating which are good and which are bad, commands humans to avoid the bad. But humans can make their own evaluations and decisions, and they may or may not obey the divine command.

There are profound philosophical disputes about whether God can know the outcome of truly free decisions before they have been made. I agree with Richard Swinburne, who has given good reasons for thinking that even an omniscient being could not know future contingent statements before they have happened.[10] This is largely for the reason that a truly free decision (in a libertarian sense) is not determined by anything in the past, not even by God. So there are events in creation that are not wholly determined by God, events that God does not even desire. That means that we cannot, to use Boethius' image, think of God as seeing the whole of time spread out before God's eternal gaze. That image implies that every element in the time-series is fully determined, and thus available for inspection. But there may be elements in the time-series that are not fully determined by any past events within the series. They may depend upon a decision that, while it may be influenced in many ways, is not determined to be exactly what it is by any past event. If that is so, we cannot envisage the whole time-series as in some way existent altogether from beginning to end, as Boethius imagined. There will be many branching pathways which may issue in very different sets of consequences. Perhaps God could see all the possibilities, but cannot know which will occur, unless God exercises such

no Karmic action

?

10. Swinburne, *The Coherence of Theism*, especially ch. 10. Richard Swinburne argues with great clarity and force, in this and other works, for many of the positions I take in the present book. Our main disagreement is on the nature of the Trinity.

God is affected by m time/space structures?

influence as will determine some outcomes to occur. I think a Christian view would be that God will determine the final outcome of the universe, and will ensure that the divine purposes for creation will be realized. But God cannot know many of the pathways that may be taken on the way to that final consummation. And it seems certain that many things will happen to which God is completely opposed.

On such a view, God has not determined, and does not know in detail the future. This is not a limitation, since if autonomous (libertarian) freedom is to exist, no being could know the future in detail. If the universe is contingent, then there must also be contingent elements in God, as God needs to respond to contingent events in constructing future states.

There are things a supremely powerful being could know about the future. Physical laws will continue to operate, laws of probability will govern what is likely to happen, and of course if God does determine that certain things will happen, then they will. The conclusion is that if autonomous freedom is real, then the universe is contingent; it could really be different than it is. And if the universe is contingent, then at least some of God's acts in the universe are contingent; they too could be otherwise, and will partly depend on the free decisions made by created persons.

Rowan Williams seems to be firmly opposed to this thought, as many theologians are. He assumes that "there is no way in which passivity can be ascribed to God."[11] No acts of God can therefore depend upon any creaturely event or act. "Something would then be admitted into the definition of what it means to be God that would be dependent on how things stood in the world," and "this would be a fundamental confusion of categories."[12] This does not seem to me to be the case. It is possible to define God, as Aristotle did, in terms that do not entail any facts about the world, and even do not imply that there is any world at all. But Aristotle's God is not the creator of worlds. If, on the other hand, you define God (partly) as "creator of everything other than itself," then something about God is dependent on how things stand in the world—namely, that there is a world created by God. If you say that the creation of a universe does not affect God's nature in any way, then you are denying that creation is a conscious and intended act of causation. If you believe the universe is created, it logically has to be admitted that God would have to be defined as one who has the ability to create a world, unlike Aristotle's God. If that ability is necessarily

11. Williams, *Christ at the Heart of Creation*, 65.
12. Williams, *Christ at the Heart of Creation*, 99.

actualized—that is, if God necessarily creates a world—that must be part of any adequate definition of God. Alternatively, if that ability exists, but is not necessarily actualized—that is, if God could create but does not necessarily do so—then there are potentialities in God. There are things that could be true of God (that he creates a universe), but whose truth depends on whether or not there actually is a universe. What is true of God (that God does or does not create) would depend on how things stand in the world—that is, on whether there is a world for anything to stand in at all.

This is not a *limiting* dependence, one that implies some lack in God. But it is a *logical* dependence, which entails that what we say about God depends logically on whether or not there is a universe, and whether God created it by an intentional act of causation.

This in itself does not seem at first to entail that there is passivity in God. But if you compare the case in which there is no universe with the case in which God creates a universe, it seems clear that God's knowledge that there is an actual universe will be different from God's knowledge that there is no universe. Therefore, the precise content of God's knowledge does logically depend upon whether or not there is a universe. God's knowledge is partly contingent if the universe is contingent, and wholly necessary if the universe is necessary. Dr. Williams says, "Humanity does not 'contribute' anything to the Godhead, and as soon as anything is said that suggests this, something essential is lost from our language about divine freedom."[13] I just cannot see this. The actual existence of humans contributes to God the divine knowledge that there actually are humans, and that God has intentionally created them. It contributes to God the actualization of a causal power to create humans, which might perhaps never have been actualized. None of this limits "divine freedom to determine our salvation," for God may still know that God has the power to bring all things to good in the end.

All these things are true whether or not humans sometimes have libertarian freedom to act without being determined to do so by God. The point is that there is nothing logically wrong or religiously inadequate in saying that the nature of God is dependent in some respects upon the existence of the universe and the nature of things in it. This simply means that either God necessarily creates the universe, and thus is necessarily a creator, or that if the universe might not have existed, then a God who creates is different from what God could have been. This entails that some of God's acts are contingent; they could have been otherwise.

13. Williams, *Christ at the Heart of Creation*, 184.

If God is really free in a libertarian sense, then there must be a state in God (presumably a quasi-mental state) at which God is able to do X or Y (to create or not to create), followed by a state in which God has chosen X or Y. This entails that something analogous to time exists in God. God will possess temporal features in the divine being itself. God's time will not be the time of our spacetime, a time where the past is lost, the future is uncertain, and the present is fleeting. It is simply a condition that allows one mental state to follow another, which allows mental change to happen. That will not be a measured time, divided into minutes and seconds. But it will be a time that allows one thought to follow another, which allows creativity and response. Its past will not be lost, its future will not be uncertain or beyond divine control—though there will be much of it that is not yet decided, and its present will not be the transient and fleeting experience that it is for us.

If God is thought of as temporal in this sense, partly to allow for the value of possessing libertarian freedom, then there is good reason to think that libertarian freedom is a good thing for temporal created minds to possess. This then entails that God must necessarily be passive to the extent that God has to wait for such finite freedoms to be exercised before God decides how to create the immediately subsequent future. This will be a perfection, not a defect, if it is thought that creative, free, and responsive relationships between minds are a positively good thing.

In Aristotle's image of a perfect divine life, God can perhaps be described as loving, in the sense that God would delight in the unchanging beauty that God contemplates. And it could be blissful, since such delight brings with it a supreme happiness. However, it could not be responsive, since there would be nothing other than God to which to respond. It could not be compassionate, since there would be nothing that was needy or sorrowful that needed comforting or strengthening. And it would not be benevolent, since there would be nothing that could be improved by its contemplative action. It is hard to see how it could be described as loving in any sense other than that of the self-contemplation of the perfect being.

PERFECTION

Aristotle did not think God was a creator of the world, since that would impair the unchanging perfection of self-contemplating supreme beauty. The idea of creation queries the Aristotelian idea of divinity. But the obvious question is, why would the perfect being create anything? More poignantly, why would it create a world containing imperfection and suffering, as this one does?

The biblical answer to the former question is that creation is of intrinsic value. What could that value be? For the Thomist view, nothing could increase the value of God, since God is perfect. But is this obvious? Dr. Williams suggests that a mutual relationship of love is a great value, which implies that there is one who loves and one who is loved, but he places these within God, as Father and Son. This proposal often leaves the Spirit with an uncertain role, as seen when Augustine sometimes thinks of the Spirit as the love between Father and Son (not a person in the same sense as them) and sometimes thinks of Spirit as one mental disposition among others (again, not a person in anything like the modern sense). The proposal can also only give a rather restricted idea of love, as both Father and Son are divine and thus unchangeably perfect. However much one speaks of this as a total and mutual self-giving, it is a love that is never in danger of rejection, that has no hint of a love of the truly other, the imperfect, the needy, or the ugly. It does not seem to be *agape* love, which is what 1 John 4 ascribes to or even identifies with God.

Dr. Williams writes, "The Trinity loves its own infinite goodness in virtue of its own eternal actuality; it cannot love any created phenomenon such as the human perfection of Jesus in the same way."[14] I think this is exactly right. God loves God's own infinite goodness precisely because it is infinitely good. If God loves created humanity, this must be a different sort of love, love of what is ontologically other.

Jesus' human nature is ontologically other than the divine nature of the eternal Word. We do not disagree here. We seem to agree also in saying that Jesus' human nature and the divine nature of the Word are united indivisibly in one compound unity (called traditionally, but very misleadingly for speakers of modern English, one "person"). So we must say that God loves the Word in one way and the human nature of Jesus in another. Analogies can always mislead, but one might think of the way in which I may love my partner as a wise and admirable politician, and also as a sexually desirable animal, but it is the same person that I love in different ways. The fact is that my partner is a socially benevolent animal, not two different people. So, we may say that Jesus is a human being, but one who is totally infused with the divine Word. The love of the Father for Jesus as human is different from the love of the Father for the eternal Son; yet in Jesus these two types

---

14. Williams, *Christ at the Heart of Creation*, 133.

of love are united. The incarnation, difficult though it is to describe—and all descriptions will be inadequate—gives the divine love a new character, which could not have existed if the Son/Word had not become incarnate.

The love of which the New Testament speaks is a love of that which is truly other than the lover, which allows that other to be truly free and self-determining, to be itself even if it disregards love. The divine love goes to the furthest lengths to reconcile those creatures who have disregarded love, and which finally includes all those who will respond (perhaps absolutely all, perhaps not) within a transfigured communion of persons, realizing the divine love itself as a redeeming, inspiring, cooperating, uniting, transfiguring power.

TRINITY

Rowan Williams hopes for the participation of humans in the trinitarian life of God. As Sarah Coakley has put it, God has a longing love for the "full and ecstatic participation in the divine Trinitarian life."[15]

I hold, and have argued at length in print, that there is no possibility of mutual love within the Trinity, because there is only one mind and will in God, so how can I construe such mutual love?[16] As I have suggested, there are different sorts of love, and one sort, love of the beautiful and good, can exist wholly within the Trinity.[17] Augustine refers to this sort of love when he uses the analogy for the Trinity of three different forms of mind. This is beatific love, divine love of the divine perfection.

But the New Testament (1 John 4) refers to a different form of love, agape love, which is love of what is other and estranged from, even opposed, to the one who loves. God loves created others, and even sinful others, and that is what the New Testament says.

For Christians, the situation is complicated by the doctrine of incarnation, which implies that a true other (the human Jesus) is indissolubly united to the divine Word. God does not just relate to this human life; God takes the humanity of Jesus into the closest possible union with God.

Given this inclusion of human life into the Trinity, there is a third form of divine love. It is, at least in this case, a union of a created being with the divine, and that can truly be called love of what is, in its own nature,

15. Coakley, *God, Sexuality, and the Self*, 10.

16. Ward, *Christ and the Cosmos*.

17. Ward, *Christ and the Cosmos*, 77ff.

other than God, but it is a love that enables that other to participate in the divine life. It is unitive love, a flowing of the divine love into a finite life, in such a way that the finite becomes part of the divine itself. It is a combination of love as relationship and love as union, as Jesus is both related to God as Father and included in the divine life as Son.

There is yet another form of the divine love, by which the divine love that is expressed in Jesus flows through him into a world that is estranged from, and often hostile to, God. It is redemptive love, which goes to any lengths to bring an estranged creation back to unity with God.

From the Father and through the Spirit, all redeemed humanity is called and empowered to be united "in Christ," and so all can be brought into a union of love with the divine. Love in its fullest sense exists in God only when God unites an estranged creation with the divine, and thus brings into being a community of love, a true union of that which is in itself radically different from the divine, which has been brought by the self-sacrificial love of God from estrangement to reconciliation, and placed within the unity of the divine life. The trinitarian God, as Christians believe God to be, is beatific, agapistic, redemptive, and unitive love. These forms of love can exist because God creates the cosmos, gives it the freedom and power to determine its own being, and brings it to its proper fulfillment by uniting it to the divine life in the most intimate way. That, I believe, is what the New Testament writer implies by saying that "God is love."

God "the Father" is utterly transcendent, hidden in the cloud of unknowing. But the Father is also the Father of Jesus, the cause of the human life of Jesus on which that human life depends at every moment, and the one who cares for the well-being and flourishing of that humanity. God "the Son" is the eternal Wisdom of God. But the Son is also expressed in and united with the humanity of Jesus from the first moment of his human life. God "the Spirit" is the dynamic life and beatific joy of the divine life. But the Spirit is also the energy that reconciles and unites the whole created universe to the divine being.

PARTICIPATION IN THE DIVINE LOVE

There is more to this story, for as one examines the nature of human persons one comes to see them as parts of a long evolutionary process, ultimately governed by a set of elegant, complex, but impersonal physical laws, and involving the gradual overcoming of difficulties and obstacles in order to achieve an eventual union with their divine source and the ultimate goal that draws them inexorably towards itself.

In the New Testament, especially in some of the Epistles and in John's Gospel, this idea of union with the divine adds something of tremendous significance to the idea of God, which is in tension with any idea of a completely changeless and impassible God. When God creates, God creates something that is other than the divine being, something that seems to be almost the complete opposite of the divine being. God is conscious; matter is unconscious. God is one; matter is many. God is purposive; matter follows laws without any apparent purpose. God is good; matter is morally indifferent.

Yet matter evolves. Guided by God, the theist would say, it produces awareness, mind, purpose, and value, and these become apparent in human beings, and perhaps in many other sorts of beings of which we are unaware. As conscious minds evolved on earth, humans became estranged from their primal source in God, and sought their own personal goods and desires rather than love of the supreme good. God then appears in various forms, symbols of the divine, to lead humans back to the Good. Christians believe that in Jesus a definitive symbol of the divine as personal wisdom and compassionate love was embodied in a human life. That symbol has become the originating source of a distinctive understanding of human purpose and destiny, that the whole of the estranged creation shall be reconciled to God.

The destiny of creation is its transformation from estrangement and alienation into an intimate union with the divine, where the whole of creation becomes a manifestation and mediation of the divine life. If this is taken seriously, it has radical implications for the idea of divine impassibility. God will not just be affected by what happens in creation. God will actually unite creation to the divine nature, and thus change the divine nature itself.

This will not be like a person putting on a coat, an image mentioned by Dr. Williams, who remarks that putting on a coat will not change the nature of the one who puts it on.[18] However, if you live in the Antarctic and do not put on a coat it will certainly change the nature of a person—that person will die. Be that as it may, uniting creation to the divine is, to use a biblical image (Isa 62:4), more like a person marrying a partner. That person will be changed, and will now live in relation and reciprocal dependence, not

18. Williams, *Christ at the Heart of Creation*, 23.

in solitude and self-sufficiency. Obviously, relations between God and created persons will never be relations of equals, since persons are completely dependent for their being upon God. But persons can receive love from God, and by their thoughts and actions they can enable the divinely given love to be expressed in new and more and relational and social forms. As the divine love is expressed in new forms, it suffers change. But "suffers" is not the right word here, for these new relational forms of love introduce new and important values in the divine being itself.

Because this is how I see the incarnation, I cannot agree with Dr. Williams when he says, "The *esse* of the Word is . . . unaffected by its union with Jesus."[19] If it is a real union, the being of each partner in the union must be affected by its union. Even if a person puts on a coat, that changes the person. It makes them warmer or drier, and that may well make them happier or more cheerful. Of course, they are still the same person, but something about them has changed. So, if Jesus is the Word-made-flesh, his humanity will, as Dr. Williams in fact says, become "aligned with" the divine love, and that is a change, a transformation. As for the Word, it will assume into itself something truly other, a human nature, and that will change the character of its love, channeling it through a human mind and senses.

This, says Williams, will not be "a supplement or an interruption but an opening into its own depths."[20] Yes indeed; but even such an "opening" to new perspectives and possibilities is a change. That change is caused by the Word, which thereby exercises a causal influence on this finite mind, whether that is conceived as an "interruption" or an "opening." I agree that "interrupting" is a misleading word, giving the impression that there is something wrong with the laws of nature, and I agree that "opening" is a helpful word, implying that finite things can reveal a reality that is in and beyond them. I agree that one should try to see finite things as disclosive of transcendent depths, and that is their true nature. But it seems to me that when that happens, those finite things can be causally transformed (not transgressed). I would be happy to speak poetically of this as the finite expressing the infinite, as Austin Farrer and William Blake did. But if it is clarity we want, I think we must add that what is here called "the infinite" is not an *absolutely* unlimited being, though it is an existent reality unconditioned by anything but itself, which has the nature of goodness, wisdom,

19. Williams, *Christ at the Heart of Creation*, 16.
20. Williams, *Christ at the Heart of Creation*, 253.

reveal, expose

and love, and which causally influences finite events as it responds to them in personal ways.

X those who are allowed to suffer?

FINITE AND INFINITE

The trouble with the word "infinite" is that it is annoyingly vague. If it means that God has no limits at all, that does not make sense. God is limited precisely by being God, by being good, wise, powerful, and loving. These are ways in which God is, and they exclude their opposites. God is not evil, stupid, weak, and malevolent.

If God is infinite, does that mean that God excludes nothing, that God includes the created world? Or does it mean that God contains nothing finite, so that God excludes the created world? Both alternatives have problems. If God includes the world, it seems that God will include evil and imperfections of many sorts. If God excludes the world, it seems that creatures could never share in the nature of God—though for many such sharing is a Christian hope. Maybe Christians want to say that the created world has its own autonomy, and is other than God. But its destiny is to become a sharer in the divine life. The term "infinite" is not very helpful here, because there is a sort of dialectical tension between the creation and the creator. Creation is estranged but reconcilable. Dr. Williams speaks of a "non-dual non-identity" between God and creation, and that seems to catch something of their relationship. However, the polarity of finite and infinite does not seem to do that. To say that the limited is other than the unlimited, but is capable of becoming part of what is unlimited, scarcely makes sense, unless it means that we shall all lose our identities in God. It seems more illuminating to say that we are deficient images of a perfectly good and wise God, and can through God's help become more perfect images and mediators of the divine life, something that Christians claim to see foreshadowed in the life of Jesus.

To many philosophers and theologians, including Aristotle and many early Christian writers, the word "infinite" connotes something indeterminate, and therefore is not adequate to a God of perfect goodness and beauty. However, I see how the word "infinite," like the word "eternal," can be used poetically to refer to what is beyond my understanding and present grasp, though it must be beyond in the sense of greater and more valuable, of offering endless (that is certainly one sense of infinite) and indestructible (the poetic sense of "eternal") forms of goodness and bliss.

Dr. Williams sometimes uses this sense of "infinity." He says, "God is infinite and beyond all categorisations."[21] In this sense, being infinite seems to mean "not capable of description," or "transcending all our descriptions." I have suggested that one should say that while God transcends all our descriptions, there are many true things that we can say of God. Thus "infinite" should not mean "totally beyond description," but "much greater than anything we can imagine"—though we can correctly say many things about God.

To take a much discussed example, one might say that God is "infinitely" powerful, meaning that God is as powerful as any being could possibly be. As a poetic expression, that is quite acceptable. But there are conceptual problems. These become obvious when one asks whether God could do something evil. It is possible to say that God could, but God will not, since God is necessarily good. However, if God is necessarily good, then God *could not ever*, in fact, do evil. God's power is limited by God's goodness. That is not bad, but good. Therefore, some limitation (some defining properties of God) must exist in God. Exactly what those defining properties are is extremely difficult, perhaps impossible, for humans to know. There may be many elements of necessity in the being of God that we cannot know. But because they must exist, it is probably better not to call God infinite, in the sense of being absolutely unlimited in any respect. It is probably safer to say that God is the most powerful being there could possibly be, rather than to insist that God is unlimitedly or absolutely omnipotent—a term that has often been used by theologians but is not found as such in the Bible.

There is certainly a distinction to be made between finite and infinite, but the trouble is that there are many different distinctions to be made between different interpretations of these terms. I suggest that by finite we could mean: bounded by space and time, and by infinite we could mean: not limited by anything other than itself, its own nature, and its own decisions. That would be a fairly clear distinction. But it leaves much hard work to be done in deciding what the infinite nature is. It is my belief that it might be best simply to say that God has a specific nature of which we truly know some things, one of which is that God is personal in making decisions about what is to exist, what the purpose of such things is, and having the power to bring about that purpose.

The Christian story of the universe is one of creation, estrangement, reconciliation, and *theosis* (sharing in the divine nature). This is a story

21. Williams, *Christ at the Heart of Creation*, 241.

that the Aristotelian/Thomist picture is in danger of missing entirely. Or, more correctly, it has never really missed it, since the mystical tradition of union with God has always been a central part of Catholic spirituality. It is a central theme in Dr. Williams own penetrating writings on spirituality. In recent years, the idea of the Trinity as a relation of persons has begun to recognize the value of love's relationality, and thereby to complicate, if not contradict, the doctrine of divine simplicity. Yet, while it does often refer to the possibility of human participation in the trinitarian life, it still resists the clear implication that such participation, if it is real, will change the life of God. One being cannot allow, or invite, another to participate in its life without that life being changed. How, it may be said, can any change in a perfect being be a change for the better? It should not be thought that God improves. It is rather that the divine nature actualizes its potential in many different ways. The actualization of the new is itself a facet of perfection, if perfection is understood, as I think it should be, as inherently dynamic and creative.

6

Incarnation and Atonement

IN CHRIST

The theme of participation in the divine life is one that has received a great deal of attention in recent theological writings. This theme has implications for the relation of divinity and humanity that have not always been followed through. There are important parts of the New Testament that entail the eventual participation of all creation in God, and they add a vital ingredient to the Christian conception of how created things relate to God.

The writer of the letter to the Ephesians says, "He [God] has made known to us the mystery of his will . . . as a plan for the fullness of time, to gather up all things in him [Christ], things in heaven and things on earth" (Eph 1:9–10).

For this writer, Jesus shows humans something new and amazing about God. He shows that God has a plan for the universe, and that plan is that everything in heaven and earth will be gathered up or united in Christ. That little phrase "in Christ" (*en tō Christō*, or often just *en Christō*) occurs many times (more than eighty-two) in the New Testament letters, and it is one of the most significant, and one of the most ignored, in Christian theology.

Whatever it means to be united in Christ, it certainly means that Christ in some way includes every created thing that has ever existed, whether

in Christ 115

angels, spiritual beings, humans, animals, plants, or planets. Christ in this sense is not just a male human being, not just Jesus of Nazareth. Christ is a reality that contains the whole universe, even perhaps many universes. Christ contains multitudes of beings.

Neither is Christ a spiritual being that exists apart from, over and above, the universe. Christ is not another separate thing in addition to all the things in the universe. Rowan Williams is right about that. Christ is that which contains the universe, the reality that is such that "in him all things hold together," as the letter to the Colossians puts it (Col 1:17).

Thus, the universe is never apart from Christ, as though it was connected to Christ as an external reality. Rather, Christ is the truest nature of reality, more than all the things that exist, but also that in which they exist. Christ is the ultimate spiritual environment in which all material things exist, the embracer of the universe.

Yet the text suggests that the unity of all things in Christ lies in the future, in "the fullness of time." It is a divine plan not yet realized. At present things are in need of reconciliation to God. They are estranged and scattered and far from the root of their being. They are held together by Christ, but have not yet attained unity with Christ. They do not realize what they truly are, or what they have it in them to become. Their potential is hidden, and they will achieve unity only when that potential is realized.

To attain that goal is the purpose of all created persons. They are to move from estrangement to union, to expand freedom by fruitful cooperation with others and to expand compassion by sharing the experiences of others. In this progress, the whole created world will be shaped into a sacrament of that perfect goodness, beauty, and wisdom that is the source of its existence. Thereby that source itself will realize a supreme goal attained through creative development in and through a communion of creative agents. The task of such agents is to realize values in the created world that have always been potential in the unlimited reality of the divine life.

The letter to the Colossians says, "In him [Christ] all things in heaven and on earth were created, . . . all things have been created through him and for him" (Col 1:16). Christ is the reality in, through, and for whom all things were created. The paragraph in which this sentence occurs contains the difficult phrase that Christ is "the first-born of all creation." The phrase is difficult because in traditional Christian thought Christ is not part of creation at all, but is uncreated and, as the Gospel of John puts it, was always "with God and was God" (John 1:1). It makes sense, however, if one thinks of Christ as the pattern of creation existing in God, like a thought in the mind of God (this is one way of translating the Greek word *logos* that John uses). Since Christ is not just an impersonal thought, but a personal reality, it might be better to say that Christ is God existing in the mode of conceptualizing intelligence. This intelligence contains the pattern or plan of the universe, and it is realized or embodied as the "container," the all-embracing spiritual reality, within which the created universe is to exist. The pattern in the mind of Christ becomes the actual ground-plan of creation.

This is a sort of first incarnation of the divine in the universe, a first outflowing of what is in the divine mind into physical reality. The creation is through Christ, because all things come into being in accordance with the divine pattern, and are formed within the spiritual reality which is the foundation of their being.

The creation is "for" Christ, because it has a future intended goal and purpose. That goal is the full realization of a community of wills bound together in cooperation and empathy, within an environment that manifests the many forms of the beauty and wisdom and power of God, and filled with the knowledge of God's presence, and the power of the divine love.

The significance of this for us is that the foundation and root of our being is not some blind and valueless assembly of material particles that just happens to throw us into existence and then as blindly and pointlessly extinguishes us again. We live within a basically spiritual reality, a reality with consciousness, value, meaning, and purpose. It intends that we should exist. It has a purpose for us, that we should find a fulfilling and worthwhile life. It can ensure that we do find such a life, even though our own small efforts often seem unable to do so.

Each of our lives has a goal, and that is to discover what is uniquely good and enduring within us, to cultivate it, and to enable it to flourish.

This is not a self-centered pursuit of personal perfection, which neglects the rest of the world in which we live. Our fulfillment lies precisely in bringing into being all the beauty and creativity that lies in the world around us, in making our world more beautiful and fruitful, in caring for the whole reality of which we are part.

Reality is not just made up of lumps of unfeeling matter, to be used in accordance with whatever desires we happen to have. It is a world that exists within the being of Christ, a life enclosed and embraced by Supreme Spirit. That Spirit gives direction and point to the way our lives go. It invites us to help our world and our lives to express more fully the life of Spirit, the life of Christ, that more abundant life to which we are called. Christ calls, Christ strengthens and upholds, and Christ fulfills the creation. Our lives are not meaningless meanderings in an uncaring universe. Our lives are created, called, and directed to be uniquely fulfilled within a universe whose innermost foundation is the Spirit of joyful and compassionate love.

JESUS OF NAZARETH

What has all this to do with Jesus of Nazareth? The plain fact is that it is his life that has somehow disclosed this vision of reality as the truth about human existence. Jesus does not point to his own humanity as the ultimate truth about reality. Jesus points to the Christ who is the firstborn of all creation, through whom, in whom, and for whom the whole universe exists, in whom all things will be united, as the ultimate truth about reality.

Jesus does not point to the Christ as one who is far away or as separated from his human life. What happens in him is something quite extraordinary. The Jewish hope for a Messiah, a Davidic king who will liberate his people from political oppression, is totally transformed into a universal hope for a supreme spiritual power who will liberate all people from spiritual oppression and slavery to greed, hatred, and ignorance. This is the Christ, the Messiah for a world estranged from its own spiritual foundation, the liberator from the spiritual slavery of the human race.

Did Jesus himself do this? We cannot be sure of exactly how Jesus saw himself. The first three Gospels present a very different picture of how Jesus spoke about himself than does the Gospel of John. In John's Gospel, Jesus speaks about himself as the light of the world, and as one with the Father. But in the first three Gospels he never says such things, and seems to be presented as a man, though a very remarkable man with divine authority and power, who is believed by his disciples to be the Davidic king who will liberate Israel from Roman oppression.

There are various ways of dealing with this difficulty, and I incline to accept the view, taken by many biblical scholars, that the first three Gospels record fairly accurately the things that Jesus is likely to have said. John's Gospel is written in a way that reads early Christian beliefs about Jesus' divine status back into the words of the historical figure of Jesus. It seems to be to this Johannine tradition that the statements about the cosmic Christ in the letters to the Ephesians and Colossians belong.

Nevertheless, in the first three Gospels Jesus does not easily fit a picture of him as a purely human prophet with divine authority. He forgives sins, he is presented as one who will return in glory to judge the world, he institutes a meal that is to be a memorial and making-present of his self-sacrifice to liberate humanity, and he appears after his death before ascending to the presence of God in glory.

Taking these things into account, I think the most plausible interpretation is that Jesus taught using the terms of Jewish thought about the coming of the Messiah and the coming of a day of judgment in which Israel would be delivered from oppression. But he forced the meaning of these terms into new and, to his hearers, cryptic forms. Thus, Mark records that he spoke in parables so that people would not clearly understand him, and the Gospels show that even his disciples continually misunderstood him.

What does seem pretty clear is that he called disciples, and sent them out to proclaim that the "kingdom of God" (perhaps a better translation would be "the rule of God") had come near. It had come near, but it was not yet fully present. The texts never explain just what the kingdom of God is, but there are plenty of hints that it is not be any sort of political organization.

If this is so, John will be correctly bringing out the hidden meaning of Jesus' teaching when he says that "the Word became flesh," even if Jesus himself never used such an expression. The kingdom, or rule, of God would be the outbreak of the divine Spirit into human lives in a new way. That way would be defined by the life of Jesus, by the compassion and moral challenge of his teaching, and above all by his self-sacrificial death and his appearances to the disciples after physical death. That human life in its totality was the model of the divine nature and of what a human life in union with that nature would be.

The Word, the cosmic Christ, could not just turn into a human being. It would always remain the foundation and all-embracing spiritual circumference of the universe. But the Word could shape some finite entity into a "non-picturing model" of its true being. Various finite parts of the universe are suitable for such modelling, some more and some less. A human life of compassion and concern for the welfare of all creatures is particularly suitable as a model or image, a physical realization, of that plan and archetype of creation, which is the Christ, the Word of God.

There is no thought here of some finite person being omnipotent and omniscient. But there is the thought that a fully human life would be enriched and expanded by a wisdom higher than its own, a power greater than its own, and a compassion deeper than its own. It would not be tormented by self-regarding desires, cognitive delusions, or emotional imbalances. It would be a life well lived and joyful, pursuing its goals with creativity and passion.

One of its main goals would be a deep and lasting relationship with the personal reality that is the mind of the cosmos, a relationship so close that it could truly be described as one of union. The human and the divine would not be conflated, leaving no difference between them. But they would be as it were intertwined, forming a compound unity that could not be broken or undermined. This would be a life not estranged from God, and thus unlike the lives of the great mass of humanity in our world.

Such a life might be possible for one who was truly and fully human, and perhaps it is a life that all persons will share when the rule of God, the communion of all persons, exists in its fullness. In this world, Jesus' life is unique, and it quickly led his disciples to acknowledge him as their Lord, as the living image of the spiritual reality which they worshipped as it was seen in and through him. In the world to come, Jesus, in his glorified form, will remain unique, as one who had the vocation to be Lord of the kingdom and the one through whom the way of eternal life in God was clarified and made accessible to all humanity.

INCARNATION AND THE TWO NATURES TRADITION

It may seem that my account of the incarnation is at odds with the main orthodox Christian account. Robert Stackpole, in *The Incarnation*, sees my account, given more fully in *Christ and the Cosmos*, as an "action Christology," which is deficient in comparison to the orthodox "two-natures Christology."

The two-natures account insists that Christ is one "person" with two natures, human and divine, but with only one subject of the very different experiences and actions proper to both natures, and that subject is, according to the Second Council of Constantinople, the eternal Word.

An action Christology holds that there are two persons, one human and one divine, and the human is so transparent to the divine that it can be taken as a finite image of the divine nature. There are two subjects of experience and action, one sense-based and limited in knowledge and power,

120

and the other purely spiritual and perfect in knowledge and power. But, Stackpole suggests, this similarity of will and purpose is not an identity, so it is not truly an incarnation, not the eternal Word itself that comes to have a human nature.

This can feel like an important difference. To say that Jesus is a man who is like God feels very different from saying that Jesus actually *is* God. I feel the emotional pull of the statement that "God himself, in the person of his Son, came among us as one of us, to share our lot and to save us."[1] God in person walked among us and gave his life to save us. However, the situation is logically quite complex. It is easy to say "Jesus is God," but very difficult to say what this could *mean*. Jesus is not omnipotent or omniscient, so he does not possess all the properties of God. This is not a simple identity, where A possesses all the properties that B possesses. Furthermore, on the traditional account, the divine Word is impassible and unchanging, so is not affected in any way by its own human nature or its sufferings. The human nature is in some sense an addition to the divine nature, but it is an addition that does not affect the divine nature.

The human nature, on the other hand, is affected by having the Word as its subject. It will have enhanced wisdom and power, and it is hard to say how much these human powers can be enhanced without contradicting the true humanity of Jesus. It will have immediate access to the mind of God, an enhanced experience of God, and an intense and constant love of God. It will be without sin and the estrangement from God that produces, and will presumably be protected from errors with regard to God and salvation. It will be an instrument of divine grace to others. It may seem that this is very similar to the robust incarnational view that, as Brian Hebblethwaite puts it, the human subject of Jesus is the "human expression and vehicle, in his incarnate life" of the divine Son.[2] In fact, I think that it amounts to the same thing. Nevertheless, on the traditional view all changes will be in Jesus' human nature; none of them in the divine nature. So does the divine subject (*hypostasis*) experience change and suffering, and thereby become affected by them? The answer seems to be: as divine, no; as human, yes. Yet if the subject is wholly divine, how can it experience change?

The dilemma is pressing: if there is a divine subject of experiences, it cannot experience change, because it is changeless, by definition. If there is a human subject of human experiences, it must experience change, it must

1. Stackpole, *Incarnation*, 655.
2. Hebblethwaite, *The Incarnation*, 31.

grow and develop, and respond to events as they happen. If there is just one subject of experiences in the incarnate Christ, it both experiences change and it does not. That is not a very happy conclusion.

It seems that even on the two-natures view there must be a human subject of changing acts and experiences. There must be some subject that is so affected, and is the "owner" of those changing and emotionally charged experiences. Otherwise Christ would not have a true and full human nature. And there must be a divine subject of unchanging divine truths. This seems to be collapsing into a two-person (or two-subject) view after all. Some philosophers (Thomas Morris, for example) call this a "two-minds" account, one limited human mind and one unlimited divine mind.[3] The divine mind knows everything the human mind knows, but the human mind, while having privileged access to the divine mind, does not know everything in the divine mind. However, it should be noted that even to give the divine mind knowledge of the contents of the human mind raises the problem of how the changeless can know the changing. It should also be noted that this is not a case of two "persons," minds, or subject of experience, of the same sort. A human mind is finite, learns gradually, reasons imperfectly, and commits many errors. God is personal, so can be rightly thought of as mind-like. But God is not just a mind, but a reality of the greatest possible knowledge and power, which does not just contingently exist, and which is beyond human power to understand adequately. God is infinite, in the sense that nothing but God limits God's nature and existence. Any reality that holds these two different kinds of thing, the infinite and the finite, together will be a compound unity, not a simple identity. One might think of it as a cooperative unity of different kinds of being, which is indivisible and necessary. Each "nature" retains what is proper to itself, yet there is a synergistic unity between them that both brings humanity to its full potential (which would include union with the divine nature), and realizes the divine nature as agapistic, unitive, and redemptive love.

Though there are two subjects of actions and experiences, admittedly of very different types, it could properly be said that the divine mind is the "ultimate subject." It brings the human mind into being and holds it in being. It makes it the case that the thoughts and acts of the human mind express the divine nature. It mediates the power of salvation through the human mind. It gives the human mind clear knowledge and intense love of God and preserves it from sin. And it identifies itself totally with the

3. Morris, *The Logic of God Incarnate*.

experiences of the human mind (takes them as "its own," not as the experiences of a separate and independent self, which it must to some extent judge and redeem).

All this is compatible with saying that Jesus, as a human mind, is, in the modern sense, a "person." That is, he has a will of his own that can make decisions and decide on courses of action (the Council of Constantinople implied as much), and who is a changing subject of temporal experiences, as all human persons are.

The divine Word is not a "person" in this modern sense, so this is not a case of there being two persons of the same sort. The Word is suprapersonal, being the one through whom all creation originates, in whom the cosmos holds together, and in whom all things will be united. God is truly personal, though God is also much more than personal, in any sense we can understand that word. In my view, the Christian trinitarian account is therefore that each "mode of subsistence" of the one mind and will of God is truly personal and more.[4] The Word is one personal mode of subsistence of the one God.

Through and by means of the personal action of the Word, God makes the human person of Jesus what it is, a unique expression and mediation of the divine nature as agapistic love to the human world. In that sense, the Word is the *hypostasis*, the basic foundational reality, of the human person of Jesus.

Jesus, as a fully human person, will receive information through his senses, will process that information through a human brain, and will make creative decisions of his own. But he will do so within the boundary conditions set by the eternal Word, which may be expected to extend his human mental and physical powers, and to implant in him a sense of his intimate and indissoluble union with the divine.

This entails that Jesus is not just a man who is like God in important ways, and neither is it helpful to say that he is God in a completely unqualified way, just like that. Jesus is a fully human person. Solely by divine grace, he is created to be "God finitely expressed in human form." God guides and empowers his thoughts and actions, and identifies with his experiences in a unique way. In him, humanity and divinity are united indissolubly, and that unity is an interaction of temporal experiences and actions with eternal values and purposes.

---

4. This is Karl Rahner's suggestion (*subsistenzweise*) for a different reading of the traditional English term "person of the Trinity"; cf. Rahner, *The Trinity*, 75.

I believe this view would be able to say that Jesus is the human form of God. God's having a human form changes humanity, for it gives it a sanctity and importance that would otherwise be hard to justify. It also changes God, or rather, realizes the being of God as a dynamic, creative, compassionate, and loving, creator of a communion of persons who unfold the divine love as beatitude, self-giving compassion, and union.

If such an account is acceptable, action Christology and two-natures Christology do not have to be opposed as exclusive alternatives. Robert Stackpole gives a beautifully clear account of them as alternatives, and shows that, in the hands of many, they are indeed exclusive. They can, however, be seen as ranged along a spectrum of possibilities that converge at a central point. My concern is to outline a position that exists at such a convergent point. In doing so my hope is to preserve the importance of human dignity, creativity and freedom; to urge a "cooperative" view of divine actions, rather than a total determination view; to uphold the thought of divine-human, or more broadly, creator-creature, union as a universal goal; to emphasize the supra-personal (but also fully personal) nature of Christ as a cosmic reality; and to suggest that God empathizes with all human pain and sorrow.

Stackpole holds, in his "new kenotic theory," that the divine Word takes the human experiences and sufferings of Jesus into the divine nature. Thus far, I agree, though I think that having genuine experiential knowledge necessitates a temporal aspect to the divine being. For a truly timeless subject cannot take temporal experiences into its being without changing their nature quite radically. For instance, Jesus' experience of abandonment on the cross could not be experienced as abandonment by the divine nature, which is incapable of abandoning itself. Human experiences may be taken into God, but there they will necessarily change their nature. So we do not quite get the sense that the divine being experiences exactly what a human being experiences, even in the case of Jesus. There is a need to preserve the sense of two coinhering kinds of subjects, divine and human, even when they are so indivisibly united that there can be said to be one *hypostasis* that unites them.

I would also want to say, as I have argued previously, that God does not only share in the passion of one young Jewish man, though God experiences what Jesus experiences in a uniquely self-identifying way. God shares in and affectively responds to the pains of *all* sentient creatures. Jesus is not the only place in all creation where God shares in the experiences of creatures. Jesus expresses in one definitive case what is true of God always and everywhere, and he expresses it in a form that is a paradigmatic but wholly human image of the divine love.

ATONEMENT

Jesus' vocation, his personal purpose, was precisely to express in a particular temporal human life the eternal nature and the universal purpose of the eternal Word. To fulfill that vocation, it was necessary that he should die and be seen to have entered into a spiritual form of existence in God. It was to be in death and resurrection that the nature of the eternal Christ would be most fully manifested in the world.

Why did Jesus have to die? The philosopher Plato foresaw the reason four hundred years before Jesus. If there was ever a truly just and good man, Plato said, he would be put to death by those whose hypocrisies and injustices he exposed by his life and teaching.[5] So it was with Jesus. The religious authorities hated him for his criticisms of their petty authoritarianism. The political authorities hated him for what they saw as challenges to their absolute power. Even many of those who followed him came to hate him because he did not offer them the advantages they sought. He was put to death as a disturber of the peace, a rebel against the authority of the religious establishment, and a potential danger to the rule of Rome. On the cross on which he died were written the words, "King of the Jews." The one who manifested most completely a wholehearted commitment to the rule of God was killed as a religious troublemaker and political nuisance.

This is what happens to love in a world lost in hatred, greed, and pride. Jesus' death was not a matter of God requiring blood as some sort of punishment for sin. It was a demonstration of what happens to love, even to divine love, when it meets the reality of pride and greed that Christians call "sin." There was a price to pay, and it was a price paid by Jesus—a "ransom," as the Gospel of Mark puts it (Mark 10:45). The spiritual reality is that God experiences the estrangement and bitterness of a world that has turned away from the foundation of its being. Christ, the eternal Word, does not remain in unchanging bliss, unaffected by the hatreds and duplicities of the human world. As Christ includes within his being the whole universe,

5. Plato, *The Republic*, Book 2, 362a: "The just man will be thrown into prison, scourged and racked, will have his eyes burnt out, and, after every kind of torment, be impaled."

which must include the experiences of all conscious beings within the universe, so Christ includes the sufferings of the innocent and the hatreds of the arrogant, the struggles of the poor and the excesses of the rich. The experiences of creatures, in all their variety and complexity, are contained within the all-embracing Christ. The image of a figure impaled upon a cross is an apt image of the way in which the sufferings and injustices of the world affect the divine life. The passion of the Christ is the passion of a God whose creation has turned away from the reality of the Good towards the destructive chaos of a world of mutually antagonistic wills.

Jesus' death on the cross is the earthly image of the passionate love of the eternal Christ for a broken world that seeks to destroy the love that gave it birth. Jesus dies, asking forgiveness for those who seek to destroy him, and feeling the desolation of a world that has sought to cut itself off from divine love. This is the temporal image of the eternal Christ, who feels all the desolation of an estranged creation, and who seeks to turn that world back to the path of self-renouncing love.

Jesus' death is an entry into the desolation of the world. But it is not a defeat. Eternal love cannot be defeated, certainly not by physical death. Jesus' death is the victory of love over the worst that evil can do to destroy it. Its message is that nothing can defeat love, but that love gains victory, not by resorting to violent retribution, but by remaining constant and unwavering in its resolve to heal and reconcile what is injured and estranged.

The cross of Jesus shows that patient endurance and indestructible passion for the welfare of all beings is a spiritual power that can face the worst that can oppose it, and resist defeat. Its victory over evil is real, not just a heroic but ultimately ineffective resistance to the power of evil, a resistance that is perhaps astonishingly admirable, yet accomplishes nothing. For the death of Jesus is a physical, not a spiritual, death.

That does not mean it is spiritually meaningless. On the contrary, in a world in which the physical manifests and expresses the spiritual, the existence of hatred, innocent suffering, and death marks the spiritual with a tragic stain. This is not a world of unbroken bliss and eternal calm. It is a world of striving, failing, enjoying, suffering, a world turbulent and dynamic, challenging and dangerous. It is a world in which Christ is the archetype, the container, upholder, and fulfiller of its many possibilities. But if all things are "in Christ," then sufferings and dangers are in Christ as well as joys and fulfillments. The mysterious verse in Colossians 1:24—"I am completing what is lacking in Christ's afflictions for the sake of his body, that is, the church"—may refer to this fact. Paul suffers for the sake of the church, and the eternal Christ accepts and empathizes with that suffering, as Christ empathizes with the sufferings of all sentient beings. But Christ takes that suffering ("the afflictions of Christ") into the unbounded bliss of the supreme Spirit. Thereby it transforms suffering into a tragic but inelim-inable part of the plan of creation, which will move through difficulty and striving to final beatitude.

In creating such a world "through Christ," God is creating a world in which tragedy is always threatening and often present. For it is a world spun from chaos and composed of a multiplicity of creatively free agents who shape the future at least partly through their own choices. In such a world, Christ does not determine all things, but seeks to guide the world towards possibilities of greater cooperation and compassion.

Jesus, as the earthly image of the cosmic Christ, manifests this guid-ance in the compassionate, healing, and reconciling acts of his life, in the demanding and yet forgiving character of his teachings, and above all in his readiness to die as a testimony to the endurance of love in a loveless world.

The atonement is not one man dying on a cross to save a few humans from eternal hell. The atonement is God's passionate involvement in the tragic history of a world trapped in selfishness, greed, and hatred. God seeks to lead that world back to union with the wisdom, creativity, and love that is the true source and goal of all finite beings.

To do that, God enters into the estranged world and seeks to trans-form the hearts and minds of men and women from within. God does this in countless ways, often in hidden and unrecognized forms. In the life of Jesus, Christians believe, God forms an open image of true divine love. Je-sus' death shows the consequence of self-centered existence, which is that it is a way of destruction and death. Jesus' resurrection shows the possibility of a new selfless existence, which is a way of fulfillment and of life.

Jesus shows the way from estrangement to life in God, and the Spirit, which was in him, enters into the hearts of those who trust in his way. He shows that God desires all without exception to turn from destruction to life, and makes it possible for them to do so.

It is true, as Christians often say, that Jesus "died for me," that he "paid the price for my sin." All Christians believe this, but not all have acknowl-edged that in doing so, he died for *all*, and paid the price for the sins of *all*. What the life, death, and resurrection of Jesus shows is that God shares in the history of the world, and wills to liberate from estrangement all who respond to the call and demand of the good, in whatever form. This is a God who creates, who grieves because of the corruptions of God's creation, but who heals suffering and who includes creatures in the divine life. This is a God with a history and a goal, a God who is unchangeable and universal in love, and whose love works actively and creatively to realize a cosmic communion of being as the fulfillment of the divine nature itself.[6]

SACRIFICE

Ancient Judaism was a religion to which sacrifice was central. There were various types of sacrifice. The "burnt offering" was the whole offering of a perfect animal, perhaps symbolizing the costly surrender of the whole of life to God. The "fellowship offering," when worshippers ate the sacrificed animal together, symbolized the possibility of sharing fellowship with God. The "thanksgiving offering" was offered in gratitude for the good things of life, and prayer that they might continue. And the "sin offerings" and "guilt offerings" expressed sorrow for wrongdoing, the intention to make restitution where possible, and a plea for forgiveness and a new start.

The sacrifices were not magic; that is, they did not bring about some objective change in the world simply by their performance. But they were believed to be divinely ordained, so that their sincere performance did express and reinforce attitudes to God of surrender, fellowship, gratitude, and repentance. They were also seen as means of conveying spiritual gifts of acceptance, forgiveness, and strength, confirming a new divinely initiated relationship to God.

The importance of the inner relationship to God was stressed by the prophet Hosea: "I desire steadfast love and not sacrifice, the knowledge of God rather than burnt-offerings" (Hos 6:6), quoted by Jesus in Matthew 9:13. The sacrifices are not enough if performed only as formal rituals; but if accompanied by inner faith they are authentic means of conveying divine love and knowledge to those who sincerely perform the rituals.

If this is correct, the sacrifice of Jesus on the cross was not a magical rite that brings about some objective change, whatever the attitudes of the believer. It was a perfect offering of surrender to the will of God and of fellowship with God. Believers can participate in this offering by making it present symbolically in bread and wine. Christians offer, not animals, but

---

6. A sensitive account of this approach to atonement can be found in Fiddes, *The Creative Suffering of God.*

the completed self-sacrifice of Christ. In doing so, they express and reinforce their submission, thanks, and repentance to God, and receive from
God the assurance of fellowship renewed and relationship reestablished.
What is important, as for Hosea, is the love and knowledge given by God.
This is the way God teaches disciples the attitudes they should cultivate if
they are to grow into the likeness of Christ, and in which God begins to
place these attitudes within them by conveying divine love and knowledge
to them.

God makes the first move, by instituting the form of the sacrifice, the
physical death of the man who manifests the divine nature and purpose, by
voluntarily giving his life in face of human evil, in obedience to the divine
will that evil should be confronted with love. Then believers are called to
repent, to express and feel sorrow for the wrongs they have done. They
are called to make some sort of restitution for what they have done. And
God responds by promising eventual participation in the divine life, and by
placing the Spirit that was embodied in Christ within them, to enable them
eventually to attain friendship with the divine.

It is true that insofar as humans are trapped in greed and hatred they
are on the way of death—that is what Calvin expressed by saying that all deserve to be punished by death. It is true that Jesus shows the way to life, and
conveys this life to those who trust in him. And it is true that he showed
this by dying for his loyalty to the Father—this Isaiah and Calvin expressed
by saying that he "takes our punishment upon him." Christ faced the greed
and hatred of humans, suffering the death to which those things ultimately
lead.

But how can the death of a man reconcile us to God? It cannot, simply
as one unjust human death amongst millions of others. However, if this
death manifests the sorrow of God in apprehending the evil in the world,
and in seeing parts of the divinely intended creation corrupted by morally
evil choices, the death of Jesus takes on eternal significance.

When the Bible says that "God so loved the world that he gave his only
Son" (John 3:16), traditional theologians have not thought that the divine
nature of the eternal Son suffered, or that God offered someone else as a
sacrifice. They have said that the impassible Word was united to a human
nature that suffered, and that was in a mysterious sense identified with God.

I think a more perspicacious formulation, consistent with the theological stance taken in this book, is to say that the human person of Jesus
suffered and died because of the evil of humanity. Because Jesus remained

faithful to God, even when faced with death, he was able to realize the divine purpose of redeeming estranged humanity. After his physical death, Jesus entered into a heavenly, glorified life, through which the saving power of God could be mediated to humanity, and through which humanity could be united in the eternal Christ. "By his bruises we are healed" (Isa 53:5)—not meaning that his suffering *in itself* heals us, but meaning that his faithfulness to his vocation, culminating in his passion and death, led to his glorification and to the completion of his role as the savior of the world.

God in the divine nature does not literally suffer or die. Thomist theologians are right to stress that. But God feels sorrow at the suffering of humanity and the partial defeat of the divine purposes for the world. God feels joy in the ultimate realization of the divine purpose, of which both finite suffering and its healing will be sublimated parts. In this way creation brings to God modes of empathetic feeling and forms of healing and reconciling action that otherwise could not exist.

It is the Spirit within that wipes away past failures and draws us to future goodness. It is the Spirit of Christ, of the one who loved in the midst of trial and suffering, and who by his own historical life showed what the eternal God does always and everywhere.

The power of the resurrection life is the power to heal and reconcile. It is the power that makes even suffering and death a path to fuller life and joy. It was manifested in the death and resurrection of Jesus, but that was not just one singular historical event, now far in the past. That event was a temporal image of the healing and reconciling power of the cosmic Christ, which exists always and everywhere, as the deepest character of our universe.

The eternal Christ does not just assimilate human experiences of suffering and injustice, leaving them unchanged. Christ acts to bring the estranged creation back to union with its divine origin and goal. That action is not occasional and intermittent. It is everywhere present. But it becomes clearer and more obviously effective at points of mediation. These are points where finite beings become, as it were, transparent to the spiritual reality of which they are a part, if an estranged part. Jesus is not only one who shows what the nature of the eternal Christ is—one in whom Christ "becomes" flesh. Jesus is also one who conveys the spiritual power of Christ, in a spectacularly transparent form. He heals bodies and minds, he forgives and he empowers his followers with his Spirit, the Spirit that is in and through him. He "baptizes with the Spirit." It is in this way that he brings the rule of

God near, into the hearts and minds of those who respond to his challenge and call.

For this trinitarian view of God, the Father is the generating source of all creation; Christ is the archetype of the cosmos; and the Spirit is the dynamic power that realizes the archetype in a myriad finite forms, and shapes them to become constituent, conscious, and creative parts of the eternal Christ.

7

Union and Apotheosis

THE BODY OF CHRIST

Christians are often referred to as "members of the body of Christ" in the New Testament. But this is often taken just to be a picturesque metaphor for the ideal closeness of fellowship between Christians. Such closeness is an ideal, and it is all too often absent from Christian churches. But being "in Christ" is much more than a matter of being friendly with other people.

There is a sense in which everyone is in Christ already, since Christ is that spiritual reality within which the whole universe is held together. But this is not a truth of which most people are aware, and it would be rejected by many, who do not consider themselves to be parts of a spiritual unity at all. If they were not in Christ and upheld in being by Christ, people would not exist at all. Yet because of pride, greed, and hatred, human beings attempt to deny and reject this spiritual foundation of their existence. They try to be self-governing and self-regarding, ignoring the wider reality and the spiritual basis on which they actually depend. They do not recognize Christ as the principle of their being, and so have no awareness of what they really are.

Because of this fact, people have to learn to exist "in Christ" in a deeper and more real sense. They have to come to self-knowledge, to see that they

132

high point culmination climax

are meant to be channels of the life of Christ in the world, working together with others to manifest the plan of creation, which is in the mind of Christ.

There is a metaphor here, but it is a metaphor of more than friendship with others. Cooperation with others is certainly part of what is meant. But that is a cooperation in carrying out a purpose that exists in the mind of Christ. This purpose is that created things should find their fulfillment by positive creative relationship with others, and by bringing into existence new forms of understanding and goodness and beauty, which are potentially present in the cosmic mind. What is there implicit is more like a signpost or architect's sketch than it is like an exact set of instructions. There is a direction or an idea of what is possible, but the exact course that is taken or the precise working-out of that possibility is left to the creative efforts of the community of finite agents.

In this way created minds contribute in creative ways to the shaping of the future. Unfortunately, many created minds have contributed in destructive ways to the human future, and have frustrated and destroyed the possibilities for good that exist in the world for which they have been given responsibility. They remain in Christ, or they would not *be*. But they are not united in Christ, for they neither work together for good, nor do they contribute positively to the flourishing of creation that God through Christ intends.

For all things to be united in Christ they would have to express the mind of Christ, fully manifesting the beauty, wisdom, and splendor of what the divine mind intends in creating the universe. The whole of creation would be shaped and ordered by created intelligent agents, who would have an intimate knowledge and love of Christ, the supreme mind and pattern of creation. They would know that they were parts of that supreme mind, through whom that mind would seek to manifest itself and its purposes. They would take the parts of the pattern that were relevant to them, and work together to place their own unique creative stamp upon them. Thus, they would form creation as a communion of minds bound together in fellowship and mutual creative action, manifesting and filling out the mind of Christ in new and enriching ways. This is, in my view, what the Gospels speak of as the kingdom of God.

Our world is very far from that ideal. It seems far from the "kingdom of God." Yet if the world has moved far from the kingdom, the Christian good news is that the kingdom has come near to it. This was the primary message of Jesus, that "the kingdom of God has come near" (Mark 1:15). It comes near in the inflowing of the Spirit of Christ into the hearts and minds of men and women.

It should not be thought that the Spirit only began to act with the coming of Jesus. As Jesus' life shows the everlasting character of God, it shows that the Spirit that filled his life, the Spirit of self-giving love, of reconciliation, and of peace, was, had been, and always would be, the active presence of God in the lives of human beings. There are no human beings anywhere who are without the divine Spirit. But the Spirit is rarely known for what it is, the divine life given to change the inner lives of created persons.

What Jesus does is to make the true nature of Spirit clear, and to mediate the presence and power of Spirit to humans in a distinctive way. Jesus was transparent to the Spirit in a unique way, and because of that he was able to mediate the Spirit in its authentic character to those who followed him. He shows it to be the Spirit which enables one to die to self in order to receive fuller life from God, the Spirit of death and resurrection, and the Spirit of true concern for the welfare of all beings in the world.

THE MEDIATION OF SPIRIT

According to John's Gospel, Jesus said, "Unless you eat the flesh of the Son of Man and drink his blood, you have no life in you; . . . those who eat my flesh and drink my blood abide in me, and I in them" (John 6:53, 55). John's Gospel contains no account of the Last Supper, when Jesus said words like these to the disciples as they ate and drank with him before his betrayal and arrest. But these words express the same thought, that the flesh and blood of Christ must be eaten and drunk in order to enter into eternal life.

It is not surprising that many disciples no longer followed Jesus after this, for it does seem a very difficult teaching. It is important to note that in the same context Jesus also said, "It is the spirit that gives life; the flesh is useless" (John 6:63). This signals that Jesus was not speaking of his physical flesh and blood, but was using these words in a spiritual sense. But the teaching is still mysterious, for what can be meant by eating spiritual flesh? I suggest that "eating" is a symbol for taking something into oneself, making it part of one's own life. What we eat, physically, gives life and vitality. "Spiritual eating" would, by analogy, be taking spiritual life that is not one's own into oneself, where it gives new life and vitality to our spiritual, our innermost lives.

Eating physical flesh is taking a substance into our bodies to give them health and vigor. Eating flesh spiritually would be receiving a spiritual life into our own inner lives to heal, renew, and invigorate them. So, to eat the flesh of Jesus is to receive the Spirit that is expressed in the person of Jesus into our inner lives, to raise them to a new level of spiritual life. The Spirit of Christ then lives in us, and we are united to Christ so that we may be said to live in him consciously and lovingly.

In the same way, to drink the blood of Christ takes blood to be a symbol of life ("of every creature, its blood is its life," Lev 17:14), so that the blood of Christ is a symbol of the life of Christ. That life in turn points to the spiritual power that was perfectly expressed in Jesus, and that can begin to shape our very imperfect lives into the image of Jesus.

As the life of Jesus disclosed the true nature of the cosmic Christ, the spirit of self-giving love, so it mediated the power of that nature, which changed the lives of those who responded to it. John does not speak explicitly of the Eucharist, a ritual meal in which bread and wine are consecrated to be the body and blood of Christ, are offered as a sacrifice to God, and are taken and eaten by those who participate in the meal. He implies that one can receive the spiritual life of Christ into one's own life by a simple act of commitment and faith. Nevertheless, the world is the manifestation of the mind of God, and some parts of the world manifest this mind in a more adequate way than others. Those parts also mediate the Spirit of God to those who are open to receive it. The human person of Jesus, in its spiritual perfection, disclosed God in a definitive way, and was able to mediate the power of God in healing those who were sick and in transforming the lives of his disciples.

According to the Synoptic Gospels, Jesus told his disciples to eat and drink in remembrance of him, and to regard their meal as a sharing in his body (his local presence) and his blood (the power which filled his life). In this way the bodily presence of Jesus in the world beyond death was to be manifested in a real way in the taking of bread and wine in remembrance of his earthly life, and in celebration of his transfiguration into eternal life.

The ritual is a manifestation of the divine self-sacrifice (of a love that shares in the sorrows of the world) and of the power of the divine life, which triumphs over decay and death. It is a commemoration of the human life that was so united to God that it accepted the experience of suffering and death as a sacrificial way of turning human hearts to God, and a celebration of the resurrection life that transformed the suffering of that life into eternal joy. It is a way of enabling those who share in the rite to die to self and to be raised to share in a more vibrant life. Thus, it is a loving memorial of the human person of Jesus, a loving adoration of the glorified and transfigured Christ, and an incorporation into the spiritual life of the cosmic Christ, the archetype and goal of all created things.

CHRIST AS PARADIGM

Paul seems to speak of "the risen Christ" and of "the Spirit of God" interchangeably. These expressions point to the inseparable unity of Christ and the Spirit. Christ, one might say, is the pattern, the archetype, and the Spirit is the power to realize that archetype in the world of matter.

These parts of the New Testament say that the archetype of our lives is not something that remains external to us, not a mere pattern we might try to follow. It is something that calls us towards its own fullness, and that actually enters into human lives to empower them to attain that fullness, each in their own unique way.

We do not literally eat the body of Jesus, a body that perished long ago as a physical reality located somewhere in our spacetime. We take into ourselves the Spirit that animated that physical body, which is the creative power of the container of the universe and the pattern of all created existence. Jesus is the way to union with that cosmic and supracosmic Spirit. It is through him that Christians discern the nature of that Spirit, and through him that they receive the power of that Spirit into their own lives.

Jesus the man did not, of course, perish, though his physical body did. He rose in a new body of spirit, according to 1 Corinthians 15, a body imperishable, incorruptible, and glorious. Is it that body that we eat? We could not physically eat a body of spirit. Yet the spirit of the cosmic Christ is mediated to human beings in and through that body. That is the finite, transfigured form in which the Spirit is discerned by us and communicated to us. In this glorified body Jesus is still the one in whom the cosmic Christ is manifested and mediated to us. He does not now suffer, but he carries the scars of suffering, and so manifests infinite suffering transformed into infinite joy. As on earth he was the physical image of the cosmic Christ, so now he is the heavenly image of that eternal Christ.

In John's Gospel, Jesus says that "unless you eat the flesh of the Son of Man and drink his blood you have no life in you" (John 6:53). This can be interpreted in a very restrictive sense, as if people who do not explicitly receive the Spirit of Christ into their lives will be excluded from eternal life. But it does not have to be taken in such a sense, and to do so would contradict those passages in John that stress that Jesus is "the Lamb of God, who takes away the sin of *the world*" (John 1:29), not just the sin of those who explicitly believe in him. In John's Gospel, Jesus also says, "I, when I am lifted up from the earth [on the cross], will draw *all people* to myself" (John 12:32).

I think the Johannine teaching is that eternal life is life in God, so that does is in fact entail knowing and loving a personal God, and being filled with the Spirit of the living Christ. All who have eternal life will therefore have taken the Spirit of Christ into their lives. They will have come to know that Jesus is the image of the invisible God and the savior of humanity from sin and estrangement from God. For that is the truth.

Yet there are many ways to eternal life, and God desires everyone to be saved (1 Tim 2:3). I think therefore that Christians should be certain that God will seek to save everyone in the ways that are appropriate for them. Christ will come to them in the face of the stranger and the oppressed, in the beauties of nature, and in the demands of justice.

Jesus is not a person in whom one has to believe explicitly for salvation to be possible. Jesus is the person who assures us that all can attain salvation—eternal life—if they are open to the promptings of the spiritual source and goal of the world, even though they are as yet unaware that these are the promptings of the cosmic Christ. Jesus is the paradigm of salvation, not one who saves only the few who know him now. They who do not now know Christ do not of course know Christ as Christ really is. Yet we must all admit that none of us yet knows Christ perfectly, and we who see Jesus as the Christ have been given a marvelous gift. Part of that gift is the humility to realize that we are all on the way towards salvation, if we are open to the promptings of goodness and truth. What Jesus shows is that there is salvation, there is eternal life, and that it is greater and more inclusive than we might have imagined. The God-intended destiny of all rational beings is to be included with all things in heaven and earth in the life of Christ, and it is there that all things will find their authentic fulfillment.[1]

---

1. The doctrine of *apokatastasis*, or universal salvation, is well outlined in Ludlow, *Universal Salvation* and in *A Larger Hope*, vol. 1 by Ilaria Ramelli and vol. 2 by Robin Parry. My own view is that salvation is conditional on repentance, which is possible and perhaps probable for all, but not inevitable. This view can be found in my *The Christian Idea of God*, chs. 18–20. David Bentley Hart's *That All Shall be Saved* is also worth consulting.

THE JOHANNINE VISION

John's vision of the cosmic Christ is epitomized in the closing speeches he attributes to Jesus in the fourth Gospel. There he outlines the extraordinary vision of the interpenetration of all things in and by God, through Christ and the Spirit.

"As you, Father, are in me and I am in you, may they [the disciples] also be in us, . . . I in them and you in me" (John 17:21, 23). So, John has Jesus say. The Father is in Jesus; Jesus is in the Father; Jesus is in his disciples, and the disciples are in Jesus and the Father. The Father, Jesus, and the disciples are in each other. What does the little word "in" mean in this context?

It certainly suggests something more than "being alongside." It most naturally seems to mean "is part of." It makes good sense to say that Christ is in the Father, since Christ is one aspect of the being of the one and only God. In a slightly different sense, the Father is in Christ in that what Christ does originates in the Father, the ultimate source of all things, and so the will of the Father is embodied in and executed by the Son. When Christ is embodied in the human person of Jesus, there arises the possibility of filial love and of paternal love, of which Rowan Williams writes so forcefully, for the humanity of Christ and the eternal divinity of the Father can be rightly seen as different entities that can be united by mutual love. Those theologians who speak of filial love within the Trinity itself compromise the unity of the mind and will of the one and only God. But I think their stress on filial love as a central theme of trinitarian belief is correct and important. It is the creation of finite persons, and the uniting of one human person to the eternal Word, that makes filial love possible, as a defining feature of God. This is indeed a love in which the Father gives the divine being to the Son, and the Son returns that love fully and without reserve, in a relationship so close that the two become one.

The humanity of Christ is itself part of the compound unity of the eternal Christ and the human nature of Jesus. The love that exists wholly within God, which I have called beatific love, does not have the form of relational love, since together the "persons" or aspects of the Trinity form one being. The incarnate Lord is a unity of finite and infinite (where finite means limited by other beings, and infinite means bounded only by its own nature). It is strictly one with God in its eternal nature and related in love to God in its human nature. Since these natures are bound together in one "person," one compound unity, Jesus has a double relationship to God the

Father, both of union and of loving filial relationship. Jesus Christ is related to the Father in a way that uniquely combines union and relationship. Jesus can say, "The Father and I are one" (John 10:30) *and* "The Father is greater than I" (John 14:28). These statements avoid contradiction only because in Jesus divinity and humanity are different aspects of one indivisible reality.

Something like this double relationship can be found, to a far lesser degree, in the lives of ordinary Christian disciples. If Christians say, "Christ in me, the hope of glory" (from Col 1:27), we mean that the Spirit of Christ is within us. Christ is undoubtedly greater than us, yet we are one with Christ. If Christ is in me, it is not as if an alien agent interrupts my normal mental processes. It is rather felt as the fulfillment of my true self and vocation, enabling me to do things that my conscious agent-self would find difficult or impossible. It is not totally unlike the feeling a composer or artist has when they feel themselves inspired by the Muse, by a power greater than them and yet present at the very heart of their being, bringing out what is latent and yet usually untapped. It is as if there is a power deeper than the conscious self that enables one to appreciate more fully, love more intensely, and act more creatively, than is ordinarily the case. It is natural to say, in the religious case, that Christ appreciates, loves, and acts through me. It is in this sense that Christ is "in" me.

It is also natural to say that I am "in" Christ. For I can become aware that I exist together with all others who respond positively to God's call, as parts of the divine life itself. That which harmonizes and unites our lives to form one coherent pattern is the divine life. In that sense one is "in" Christ, parts of one spiritual society of cooperating agents.

Pulling all these strands together, Christians can speak of Christ in at least six main and interrelated ways. First, there is *Christ the archetype*, God as divine intelligence, embodying the thought that is the plan of creation, through which the universe is created.

Second there is *Christ as the spiritual reality within which the whole universe is held together*, the "container" of the cosmos, the "first-born" of creation.

Third there is the *Christ who is embodied in the human person of Jesus*, the temporal image and mediator on earth of the cosmic archetype.

Fourth there is *Christ as Jesus in transfigured and glorified form*, the forerunner of all those (all those denizens of this planet, though there may be many other glorified finite forms of Christ) who will be fulfilled in a renewed and transfigured creation.

Fifth, there is *Christ as the one whose "body" is the church*, those elected to witness to the self-giving and universal love of God, who live "in Christ."

Sixth, there is *Christ as the one in whom the whole universe will be united*, the achieved goal of creation, in which the archetype has been filled out and completed by the creative and cooperative acts of finite minds.[2]

THE PASSIONATE GOD

I have wanted to honor the insights of those Thomist-influenced theologians who have written profoundly about the immensity and uniqueness of God. Their work should forever eliminate over-anthropocentric images of God, which seek to subsume God completely under some human set of concepts. But they leave a major problem that if God is not describable in any human concepts, there remains *nothing* that one can say about God.

This problem can be clearly seen in the work of John Hick, who holds that what he calls "the Real" "cannot be said to be one or many, person or thing, substance or process, good or evil, purposive or non-purposive."[3] He follows this up by postulating that the many diverse characterizations of Ultimate Reality in different religions are not adequate to depict the Real; and they can all be regarded as more or less equally authentic paths to "Reality-centeredness."

This does not follow at all; for if we know *nothing* of the Real, we cannot possibly know whether any of our characterizations of it are authentic or not. Indeed, we cannot know whether there is "a Real" to which they all refer. This points up the problem of how it is that Christians can call God one and good and a purposive creator, if God is so far beyond all our concepts that God might equally authentically be called many, evil, and without any purpose at all.

Aquinas sought to bridge this problem by saying that we could use words of God analogically. This hardly works as a solution, for if God is beyond the reach of all human concepts, then God is beyond all analogies too. Analogies are, after all, human concepts, and why should we prefer some analogies to others, if none of them really apply to God?

What we need to say is that some human concepts do really refer truthfully to God, but they need not and should not be taken to give a complete

2. Ward, *The Mystery of Christ* has a series of prayers and meditations on these themes.

3. Hick, *An Interpretation of Religion*, 246.

or adequate idea of God. We are quite familiar with such uses of language in ordinary life. We can say that human beings are primates, and this will be straightforwardly true, not analogical. But if we think that is all humans are, we will have missed out something of critical importance. So, if we say that God is one, good, wise, and purposeful, what we say might well be straight-forwardly true. But it only tells us some things about God. There remains much of God that we cannot describe, and it is of critical importance that in those respects God remains beyond all human understanding.

We need to be clear, however, that this trans-categorial being of God does not contradict that of God that can be described, however inadequate-ly, in human categories. We cannot say, for example, that we think of God as good and wise, but he "not really so." God *is* truly good and wise; but God is *also* such that there is much we cannot comprehend in words. And we need to be clear that what is beyond concepts cannot be described. There is nothing we can say of it, though it may be possible in some way to ap-prehend it non-conceptually. We should not say that the trans-categorial is the "true" God, for the whole notion of truth—of statements in some language—falls away at this point. We shall have to say simply that there is much that we can understand of God, and there is much that we can-not understand. When we say that God is trans-categorial, we can then say that this is the same God as the God who is also one, wise, and good. We say that just because we know that God is much greater than anything we can describe, not because we can compare the indescribable God with the describable one and see that they are the same.

However, the problem of describing God accurately comes to the fore again when theologians attempt to use the philosophy of Aristotle as a model for speaking of God. When Aquinas speaks of God, in the *Summa Theologiae,* he follows Aristotle's arguments in the *Metaphysics* and else-where, for the existence of a perfect reality who is fulfilled in the changeless contemplation of the divine perfection. Aristotle's God is not the creator of the universe, and probably does not even know the physical universe or play any causal role in its existence (except the passive role of functioning as an ideal "final cause" to which things in the universe are attracted). But when in the "five ways" Aquinas sets out the nature of God, using Aristotle's types of causality as his guide, he faces a major problem.[4]

The problem is that the Christian God is a purposive creator of the uni-verse, who knows and loves the universe, and who wishes to unite things in

4. Aquinas, *Summa Theologiae*, 1a, 2, 3.

141

the universe to the divine being and make them participants in the divine nature. In the "five ways," Aquinas draws the picture of God as a necessarily actual cause of everything other than itself, who is of the greatest possible intrinsic value, the "most noble" of beings, and who wills a good purpose for creation, and so is "someone with awareness and understanding." This is not really compatible with saying that we do not know what God is.

DIVINE PROPERTIES

As he goes on to spell out the nature of God in questions 2–11 of the *Summa*, Aquinas argues that God is eternal, simple, infinite, changeless, perfect, impassible, and incomprehensible. It is at this point that he states that "we cannot know what God is, but only what he is not,"[5] so he is considering "the ways in which God does not exist."

This at once raises the question of whether the ways in which he says God does not exist conflict with the positive beliefs Christians have about God's knowledge and love of the universe and God's causal activity in uniting the universe to the divine. My argument throughout this book has been that in many interpretations they do so conflict. Wholly negative interpretations of these divine properties deprive the more positive assertions of God's knowledge and love of creation of their meaning.

The most obvious case is that of divine simplicity. As a statement of what God is not, this asserts that God is not complex, or made up of parts. The trouble is that there are weaker and stronger interpretations of this assertion. The strongest interpretation says that there are no distinct properties in God (mental or physical parts), that God is not in space or time (which are divisible into parts), and that God's will is identical with God's essence (there can be no distinctions in God).

If this is true, it immediately follows that God cannot change (which would involve temporal succession), cannot be changed by anything other than God, and cannot be temporally involved with the universe. The declaration that we cannot say certain things of God now threatens to conflict with some positive assertions that seem to be involved in Christian faith, such as that God creates the universe, but need not have done, or listens to and responds to the prayers of created beings.

Fortunately, there is a weaker interpretation of divine simplicity, which is that in God the central properties of the divine being are indissolubly

5. Aquinas, *Summa Theologiae, prima pars*, 1a, intro. to qu. 3.

connected. The best analogy here is that of mental consciousness, in which there are many diverse elements (perceptions, sensations, thoughts, and feelings), but all of them are parts of one consciousness that is itself indivisible and not capable of being split into separate and simpler pieces of consciousness.

This analogy suggests that conscious mind is perhaps the most adequate description of the God insofar as we can describe God. Aquinas' "five ways" corroborates this. While the first three ways do not explicitly mention any mental or personal properties, the last two certainly do. In the fourth way God is said to be the most noble and best of beings, and in the fifth way God is said to possess awareness and understanding. A noble and good being with awareness and understanding is certainly a mind, or, if more than a mind, certainly possesses mental properties. This thought enables us to give a weaker interpretation to the other features of God outlined by Aquinas. Consider:

- *God is eternal*, not in the strong sense that God has no temporal properties, but in the weak sense that God is beyond this spacetime, which allows the possibility that the being of God may include this spacetime, and that there may be a divine time that is different in character from our spacetime.

- *God is infinite or limitless*, not in the strong sense that God can contain no finite parts, but in the weak sense that God is not limited by any other being than God and what God creates.

- *God is changeless* in the divine possession of the greatest possible love, wisdom, power, and knowledge, but not in an inability to change in any respect.

- *God is impassible* in not being subject to injury or death, but can be passionately affected by what happens in creation.

In this way the Thomist stress on the uniqueness of the divine being can be protected, and be more clearly shown to be compatible with the personal nature of God, which is so important to much Christian devotion.

I have also, and most importantly, wished to argue that it is not enough to regard God as a personal being who simply stands in some external relation to finite persons. This is one reason why some theologians speak of God as "Being" rather than as *a* being, or *a* person. Unfortunately, "Being" is a very impersonal and perhaps vacuous expression, and undermines the ascription of █████ operties to God. It is better, in my view, to say that God is personal, is also transcendent to all personal and describable qualities, and is also, in a unique way, one with created reality. This would be a truly trinitarian or threefold characterization of the divine.

For many it raises the specter of pantheism, of simply identifying God with the universe. But any form of pantheism would ignore the transcendent and personal aspects of the divine being. One must therefore be careful of the sense of "identity" that is at issue if one speaks of an identity of God and the creation.

I have argued that the expression that the New Testament most often uses in this connection is the expression "in Christ." I have suggested that we should take seriously the thought that the purpose of God in creation is to unite all things in heaven and earth, all things in creation, in Christ. The universe "holds together" in Christ (Col 1:17, *ta panta en autō synestēken*). Its destiny is to come to conscious understanding of its unity in Christ. Jesus is the foreshadowing of this destiny. As his disciples, Christians are the body of Christ, and their vocation is to make this destiny known and desired in an estranged world. The universal hope is that all creation, each thing in its own way, should consciously share in the nature of God (2 Pet 1:4).

This is not pantheism, a view which simply identifies God with the whole universe. It rather seeks to include the universe within the transcendent being of God. This is obviously not a spatial sense of "in"—we are not inside God like a heart in a body. It suggests that our acts can express the actions and purposes of God (St. Teresa of Avila said that we are the hands and feet of God), and that our feelings and experiences contribute something of importance to the life of God. In a sense God acts and experiences in new ways in and through us.

If this were true, it would give a very positive meaning to creation, and a very strong sense of personal purpose to every finite life. Creation would realize new values through the actions of finite persons in cooperation with God. Those values would be incorporated into the life of God, never to be lost. And the Christian faith sets before us the hope that we shall share in that divine life. God's love is completely realized through the establishment of a communion of finite persons who have been led by Christ and the Spirit to be liberated from self-centeredness to become the receivers and transmitters of eternal love in the finite forms of a transfigured space and time. This, for me, is the "kingdom of God," which has "come near" in and through Christ, as a reality into which human persons can enter now, though its full fruition lies beyond the inexorably decaying time of this cosmos.

The major problem is that of the estrangement of humanity from God. We do not want to say that God sins in and through humans, or that God actually feels the perverse pleasures of murderers and sadists. There is also the fact that if humans are truly free to any extent, their actions must be rooted in *their own* wills, not just being no more than channels of God's will. And the laws of nature, which largely appear to be blind to moral concerns, and give rise to earthquakes and floods, are also not easily construed as direct acts of God, whatever insurance companies may say.

There is a real "otherness" about the universe and about humans in relation to God. It would be wholly misleading to say, "All that I am, just as I am, is divine, for I am part of God." The obvious way to take account of these points is to say that having the universe as the expression and mediation of the divine being is an ideal *goal* for the universe, but it is a goal *not yet achieved.* Jesus is a foreshadowing of this ideal, but his death in this world shows the extent of the gap between the ideal goal and the present reality.

This is a point at which human concepts of God are unable to grasp with any hope of fully adequate understanding the relationship between God and creation, though they are not thereby contradictory. It is rather that human concepts are so inadequate to speak of God that seemingly opposed concepts can in some cases both be seen as necessary to an understanding of God. They avoid contradiction by being incomplete, and thus by signaling that they could be reconciled in a higher synthesis, which is not, however, graspable in any known human form of thought. On the one hand, the created cosmos is not a reality totally other than God, for it only subsists in and through God, and is only held in being by God. God is the center of its being and the substance of its reality. On the other hand, many beings in the created cosmos are estranged from God, frustrate the divine will, and seem to have their own autonomous wills that are set against God.

The philosopher Hegel struggled with this problem, and spoke of God (*Geist*) becoming "other" and yet of that otherness being part of the self-realization of the divine.[6] The theologian Jürgen Moltmann, no doubt influenced by this, spoke of an internal conflict within the trinitarian being of God, whereby the Son was abandoned by the Father—expressed by Jesus'

---

6. Hegel, *Lectures on the Philosophy of Religion*, vol. 3, 170.

cry of dereliction on the cross—and yet also reconciled to the Father.[7] I am not disposed to accept such an internal conflict within the Trinity, because of my firm adherence to a monotheistic faith. But it does seem that God gives rise to and supports a cosmos that is other than and estranged from God, while that cosmos yet wholly depends upon God for its existence, and its destiny is to realize its true unity with God.

God is a supreme mind that is different in kind from any finite minds, because of the uniqueness of its relationship to such minds. Could there be "other minds" that are actually "within" or parts of this supreme mind? Not if they were closed off from one another. But what if they were wholly open? A form of cooperative action and experience would, I think, be possible. Finite minds could be channels of God's actions, in cooperation with their own creative decisions. God would act in ways in which God would not have acted without the existence of creatures. They could be instruments of God's experiences, modified in God by the co-existence of many finite minds, and by the overwhelming beauty and beatitude of the divine mind. God would experience states that God would not have experienced without the existence of creatures.

Whether these things are adequately captured by saying that "the cosmos is the body of God" depends on how one interprets that phrase. In the history of religious, the phrase is definitively associated with the twelfth-century Indian philosopher Ramanuja. He meant by a "body" something that was completely under the control of its mind, whereas we know only too well that bodies can fail to be under mental control, and can limit the capacities of minds. It is true, however, that a body is the means by which experiences reach the mind, and is also the means by which minds perform actions in the world. We can readily conceive that the experiences of finite creatures can influence the experiences of God, and the actions of finite creatures can enable God to act in new, temporal, ways. I would want to speak of a "synergy" of divine and human experiences and actions, whereby each adds something to the other—though obviously any and all human additions to the life of God are only a miniscule feature of the divine life. The Bible puts this well in speaking of a human "participation" in the divine nature. My central argument is that any such participation, if it is real, will change the divine nature, and that this will be a manifestation of the perfection of God, not a diminution of divine sovereignty.

7. Moltmann, *The Trinity and the Kingdom of God*, 80ff.

Rowan Williams writes affirmatively of a "non-dual non-identity" between God and creation. If this means that creation is not a reality independent of and separated from God, yet is also something the divine love has in part to overcome and wholly to transform, it seems to depict a sort of alienating and reconciling dynamic process *as a feature of the divine life itself.* That is why I find it strange that Dr. Williams is reluctant to speak of God as a creatively changing reality that in some sense includes the spacetime cosmos within itself, expresses part of the divine nature in particular events within that spacetime, and has the positive purpose of realizing new and unique values within spacetime that will be incorporated into the divine life, and perhaps, given the Christian hope of eternal life with God, shared by all personal beings who have lived within spacetime.

Finite agents who are or who are destined to be "in Christ" add finite experiences to God, which obviously God would otherwise not have, of which God has affective knowledge and to which God responds passionately. Jesus the Christ expresses the divine love in ways that otherwise would not exist, and unites humanity and divinity in an indissoluble way. The Spirit is an active spiritual power within finite agents, adding to them power, wisdom, and love, which they would otherwise not have. These are three modes of subsistence of one God, as God generates the universe, manifests in finite form within it, and works within finite conscious beings to unite them to the divine life. This makes it seem central to a Christian idea of God that God is not solely a changeless and timeless reality, though there is indeed a changeless and timeless aspect to the being of God. God is also, and crucially, a dynamic, interacting, power passionately and creatively involved in the world.

It is this God who, in Christ, is reconciling the world, already "held together" in Christ but now estranged from its own deepest reality, drawing the world towards a conscious and loving relation to and union with the divine life.

CONCLUSION

If this is so, there is a new and distinctive metaphysics of the Christian faith. It grounds the physical universe in a deeper and self-existent spiritual reality. Personal beings within the universe, gifted with freedom and a measure of self-determination, can realize distinctive values of creativity, development, and relationship. Unfortunately, they can also realize possibilities of greed, pride, and hatred, and often lose the sense of their spiritual roots. But the transcendental ideals of truth, beauty, and goodness remain objectively demanding, and the divine Spirit cooperates with finite minds to reinforce those ideals and help to realize them within the finite universe. There is a spiritual purpose and goal for the universe, which is the full realization of goodness and true well-being, and the defeat of evil and inordinate self-will. Spirit will then be fully manifested as love in and through many communities of finite minds, and finite minds will achieve their proper fulfillment in a communion of being with one another and with Supreme Spirit.

Within this metaphysics of objective moral purpose, human beings have a small but important part to play as they seek to renounce the evils and to pursue the values that are possible for them in their own unique historical situations. This metaphysical view is of universal significance, and can be seen to be manifested in rather different ways in many religious and ethical traditions.

Christians believe that Jesus discloses to human beings the nature of Spirit as love, can mediate the power of Spirit to enable them to participate in the divine nature, and plants in them the firm hope that they may share in the fulfillment of all things in God. This is not a metaphysics of idle speculation or mere theory; it is a foundation for living by eternal values in a world that so often seems filled with hatred and perplexity; it is a metaphysics of moral demand and promise, and as such it is a metaphysics of existential and life-changing importance.

Bibliography

Aquinas, Thomas. *Summa Theologiae.* Online, http://www.newadvent.org/summa/.

Barton, John. *The History of the Bible: The Book and Its Faiths.* London: Allen Lane, 2019.

Burrell, David. "Distinguishing God from the World." In *Faith and Freedom: An Interfaith Perspective,* 3–19. Oxford: Blackwell, 2004.

Coakley, Sarah. *God, Sexuality, and the Self: An Essay "On the Trinity."* Cambridge: Cambridge University Press, 2013.

Creel, Richard. *Divine Impassibility.* Cambridge: Cambridge University Press, 1986.

Dionysius. *Pseudo-Dionysius: The Complete Works.* Translated by Colm Luibheid. Mahwah, NJ: Paulist Press, 1987.

Ellis, Fiona. *God, Value, and Nature.* Oxford: Oxford University Press, 2014.

Fiddes, Paul. *The Creative Suffering of God.* Oxford: Clarendon, 1988.

Gregory of Nyssa. *On the Soul and Resurrection.* In *The Nicene and Post-Nicene Fathers,* vol. 5, translated by A. H. Wilson. Edinburgh: T. & T. Clark, 1988.

Hart, David Bentley. *The Beauty of the Infinite: The Aesthetics of Christian Truth.* Grand Rapids: Eerdmans, 2003.

———. *The Hidden and the Manifest: Essays in Theology and Metaphysics.* Grand Rapids: Eerdmans 2017.

Hebblethwaite, Brian. *The Incarnation: Collected Essays in Christology.* Cambridge: Cambridge University Press, 1987.

Hegel, G. W. F. *Lectures on the Philosophy of Religion, vol. 3.* Edited by Peter Hodgson. Berkeley, CA: University of California Press, 1985.

Heschel, Abraham. *The Prophets.* New York: Harper and Row, 1962.

Hick, John. *An Interpretation of Religion.* London: Macmillan, 1980.

John Paul II. *Fides et Ratio.* 14 September 1998. Online, http://www.vatican.va/content/john-paul-ii/en/encyclicals/documents/hf_jp-ii_enc_14091998_fides-et-ratio.html.

Kant, Immanuel. *Critique of Pure Reason.* Translated by Normal Kemp Smith. London: Macmillan, 1952.

Kerr, Fergus. *Theology after Wittgenstein.* Oxford: Oxford University Press, 1986.

Kneale, William, and G. E. Moore, eds. "Symposium: Is Existence a Predicate?" *Proceedings of the Aristotelian Society,* vol. 15 (1936).

Knepper, Timothy. *Negating Negation: Against the Apophatic Abandonment of the Dionysian Corpus.* Eugene, OR: Cascade, 2014.

Kretzmann, Norman. *The Metaphysics of Theism.* Oxford: Clarendon, 1997.

Kretzmann, Norman, and Eleanor Stump. "Absolute Simplicity." *Faith and Philosophy* 2.4 (1985) 353–91.

Lindbeck, George. *The Nature of Doctrine: Religion and Theology in a Postliberal Age.* Louisville, KY: Westminster, 1984.

Ludlow, Morwenna. *Universal Salvation: Eschatology in the Thought of Gregory of Nyssa and Karl Rahner.* Oxford Theological Monographs. Oxford: Oxford University Press, 2000.

Macquarrie, John. *Principles of Christian Theology.* London: SCM, 1966.

Malcolm, Norman. "Anselm's Ontological Argument." *Philosophical Review* 69.1 (1960) 41–62.

Marcel, Gabriel. *The Mystery of Being.* Translated by G. S. Fraser. London: Harvill, 1951.

Moltmann, Jürgen. *The Trinity and the Kingdom of God.* Translated by Margaret Kohl. London: SCM, 1981.

Morris, Thomas V. *The Logic of God Incarnate.* Ithaca, NY: Cornell University Press, 1986.

Parry, Robin A. *A Larger Hope? Universal Salvation from the Reformation to the Nineteenth Century.* Eugene, OR: Cascade, 2019.

Phillips, D. Z. *Death and Immortality.* London: Macmillan, 1970.

———. *Wittgenstein and Religion.* London: Macmillan, 1993.

Pinnock, Clark, Richard Rice, John Sanders, William Hasker, and David Basinger. *The Openness of God: A Biblical Challenge to the Traditional Understanding of God.* Grand Rapids: IVP, 1994.

Plato. *The Symposium.* Translated by Walter Hamilton. London: Penguin Classics, 1951.

Przywara. Erich. *Analogia Entis: Metaphysics—Original Structure and Universal Rhythm.* Translated by John Betz and David Bentley Hart. Grand Rapids: Eerdmans, 2014.

Rahner, Karl. *The Trinity.* Translated by J. Donceel. London: Burns and Oates, 1979.

Ramelli, Ilaria. *A Larger Hope? Universal Salvation from Christian Beginnings to Julian of Norwich.* Eugene, OR: Cascade, 2019.

Soskice, Janet Martin. *Metaphor and Religious Language.* Oxford: Oxford University Press, 1985.

Stackpole, Robert. *The Incarnation: Rediscovering Kenotic Christology.* Leicester, UK: Chartwell, 2019.

Swinburne, Richard. *The Coherence of Theism.* Oxford: Clarendon, 1977.

Turner, Denys. "Apophaticism, Idolatry and the Claims of Reason." In *Silence and the Word: Negative Theology and Incarnation*, edited by Denys Turner and Oliver Davies, 11–34. Cambridge: Cambridge University Press, 2002.

Ward, Keith. *The Christian Idea of God.* Cambridge Studies in Religion, Philosophy, and Society. Cambridge: Cambridge University Press, 2017.

———. *Christ and the Cosmos: A Reformulation of Trinitarian Doctrine.* Cambridge: Cambridge University Press, 2015.

———. *Holding Fast to God: A Reply to Don Cupitt.* London: SPCK, 1982.

———. *More Than Matter? What Humans Really Are.* Oxford: Lion Hudson, 2010.

———. *The Mystery of Christ: Meditations and Prayers.* London: SPCK 2018.

———. *Religion and the Modern World: Celebrating Pluralism and Diversity.* Cambridge: Cambridge University Press, 2019.

———. "Stewart Sutherland: An Appreciation." *Religious Studies* 34.4 (2018) 249–62.

Weinandy, Thomas G. *Does God Suffer?* London: T. & T. Clark, 2000.

Westermann, Claus. *What Does the Old Testament Say about God?* London: SPCK, 1979.

Williams, Rowan. *Christ the Heart of Creation.* London: Bloomsbury Continuum, 2018.

Wittgenstein, Ludwig. *Culture and Value.* Translated by Peter Winch. Oxford: Blackwell, 1980.

Index of Names

Index of Topics

Made in United States
North Haven, CT
28 March 2023